DANGEROUS
PRAYING

DANGEROUS
PRAYING

Inspirational ideas for individuals and groups

DAVID SPRIGGS

Scripture Union, 207–209 Queensway, Bletchley,
MK2 2EB, England.
Email: info@scriptureunion.org.uk
Internet: http://www.scriptureunion.org.uk

ISBN 1 85999 335 4

British Library Cataloguing-in-Publication Data
A catalogue record for this book is available from the
British Library.

Cover design by Julian Smith.
Printed and bound in Great Britain by Creative Print and
Design (Wales), Ebbw Vale.

CONTENTS

PREFACE

Four years ago, a man from Canada came to see me in my office in London. I didn't know him and was wondering why I was seeing him at all! I was Head of the Prayer Department for the Evangelical Alliance at the time, and part of the deep longing of my life was to see prayer and evangelism operating in partnership like a husband and wife. As I mulled over with God why it was that I had agreed to meet this man, I sensed God saying that he would be an answer to my dream.

To be honest, when my Canadian visitor came in, I was not convinced. However, as our conversation proceeded, I got more and more excited. The way forward became clearer, and that visit led eventually to the launching of Community Prayer Cells, a very effective process for bringing prayer and evangelism together.

It is experiences like these that make prayer so exciting for me. Whether it is pleading with God that he will bring to fruit the dreams he has fostered within me, or involving him in situations that puzzle me, I always have this sense of exhilaration. When I see him fulfil his promises or achieve the almost impossible, it seems to me that prayer does indeed deserve to be described as a great adventure.

Perhaps nowhere in the New Testament are we given more insights into the opportunities prayer offers than in

Paul's letter to the Ephesians. Of course no book, ancient or modern, even a canonical one, contains all prayer's possibilities. But this brief epistle expands and hints at many of its vital dimensions. We will look at three main passages. They are:

- Ephesians 1:15–23 (Section 1 of this book)
- Ephesians 3:14–21 (Section 2)
- Ephesians 6:10–22 (Section 3)

However, there is a fourth passage, or, in terms of the letter, a primary one – Ephesians 1:1–14 (Introduction) – which sets out the personal and cosmic boundaries within which prayer operates. In itself, this passage is neither prayer nor encouragement to pray, but it describes the source out of which prayer flows. Its vision generates the thrill of anticipation we should expect as we set about praying.

Important and wonderful as prayer is, it is not the whole of our relationship with God (not unless we define prayer so loosely, that it covers virtually every aspect of the Christian faith). Yet prayer has such profound consequences on our lives. Answers to prayer flow back into our experience, bringing delight, amazement, awe and sometimes perplexity. Such answers give zest to our praying, but they are not the whole of prayer either. Central is our growing relationship with God and, through God, with others.

This is what makes Ephesians so rich. Throughout Paul's prayers here, and the hints he gives us about praying, there shines an authentic relationship with God which makes me long to know more of Paul's kind of prayer life. In fact, in Ephesians there are no 'answers to prayer' as such, although no-one could pray as Paul does who does not know that God answers prayer. Indeed, the pivotal verse of the whole letter is a confident affirmation of that fact:

> 20 To him who by means of his power working in us
> is able to do so much more than we can ever ask for,

or even think of: [21] to God be the glory in the church
and in Christ Jesus for all time, for ever and ever!
Amen. *(Ephesians 3:20–21)*

We will return to these two verses at the end of the book,
but for now I invite you to let them flow through your
mind, exciting your heart and igniting your spirit. They
are intensely personal. God is, at this very moment, at
work in each Christian – yes, *in us.* And yet the vision of
these words is so vast in its scope – for all time, for the
whole church and, above all, for the glory of God.

So, before we embark on this exploration of prayer
together, it would be helpful to glean some sense of the
importance of the journey we are about to undertake. If
possible, please read these two verses a few times quietly
to yourself. If you are in a small group, read them out loud
in turn, perhaps using different translations, with a
moment of quiet between each reading. Maybe, having
done this, you will find yourself wanting to respond with
your own prayer or enjoying a deep silence of communion.
If you have creative gifts, a poem, a painting or even a
piece of music may be your way of expressing your
response to this vibrant doxology. Whatever you do, take
time to reflect on the wonder of the God Paul is describing.

You will by now have discerned that this book is not
setting out to be an intellectual exposition on a few passages in Ephesians. Nevertheless, it depends on such
intellectual awareness and I want to affirm the value of
keen minds, for they are also a gift from God.[1] However,
this book is primarily concerned to help people grow in
their relationship with and enjoyment of God through
prayer.

The more detailed exploration of the passages will
focus on some key themes relating to prayer and to our
relationship with God. This will be rather like following a
track through a wood when we are on a walk. Any particular track will intersect with others or even cross the main
route further along. So, as we explore these themes, we

will sometimes find ourselves moving across all four main passages. We may then return to base to explore a different path. Eventually we will move base and see what fresh vantage point another passage has to offer.

Because I am concerned to create a biblically informed context in which people can discover more about God through prayer, and because such discovery is more than simply a mental awareness of the possibilities, I have included suggestions as to how people might be part of the adventure rather than remain spectators from the sidelines. So at the end of each chapter there is a variety of ways to explore and apply Paul's insights for ourselves. It seems to me that we will not have done justice to his open-heartedness, both to God and to his readers, until we have integrated his perceptions into our living and relating.

Recently, I came across a helpful distinction between 'consumers' and 'creators' of meaning. If we read someone else's explanation and just accept it, then we are 'consumers of meaning'. If we absorb it and fit it into our own lives, thus reshaping our lives around the truth, then this is one way that we can become 'creators of meaning'. The intention of this book is that readers will become active partners in building truth into their own lives as they respond to the perspectives I am about to share.

There are a multitude of ways in which this book can be used. It could provide a series for house groups during Lent or after Pentecost, or during the summer (or, indeed, all three, using one section of the book for each short series). Each section could be introduced by an exposition of the key passage during a main service, thus encouraging more people to go to the house groups.

If your church is moving towards adopting the cell church approach, then Section 3 (or 3.3, plus the Appendix) would help to develop a 'mission heart' for the cells. Each cell could be asked to implement one of the prayer strategies for the longer term.

A valuable alternative for some churches might be to

have an 'away day', and make use of selected chapters, such as 1.2, 2.2, 2.3, to form the basis of the day. Alternatively, the church could commit itself to broadening its repertoire of prayer within the worship service or at a central prayer gathering. If people feel too threatened by this, then the different styles could be tried within the security of smaller groups, followed by a meeting at which people shared their experiences.

Whatever you decide, there are huge benefits in sharing this book and its ideas with other Christians. Indeed, the book began as a series of talks for a church in America. The preparation, the occasion of delivery, and the outcomes for the church as well as myself, have shown all involved that to engage with these prayers of Paul is to enter a realm of blessing and growth.

This journey in prayer may seem dangerous. We cannot predict where it will take us, what new things we will see, who we will meet, what decisions we will take, how we will be at the end of it. What we can be sure of is that we will be different and our relationship with God will be enriched beyond measure.

Why am I so sure of this? There are two main reasons. The first is to do with the quality and relevance of the biblical material that we will be looking at together. These passages from Ephesians reflect the practice and insight of one of God's greatest saints at the peak of his maturity, a maturity forged through costly obedience, passionate spirituality and incredible missionary experiences, all imbued with deep theological reflection and complete trust in God. These prayers are themselves the spoils of Paul's adventure with God.

The second reason for my confidence is that God's Spirit will be intimately involved with us throughout our journey:

The Spirit is the guarantee that we shall receive what God has promised his people... *(Ephesians 1:14)*

I remember you in my prayers and ask the God of our Lord Jesus Christ, the glorious Father, to give you the Spirit, who will make you wise and reveal God to you, so that you will know him. *(Ephesians 1:16–17)*

Introduction: Ephesians 1:1–14
FROM PLAN TO PRAISE

[1] From Paul, who by God's will is an apostle of Christ Jesus –

To God's people in Ephesus, who are faithful in their life in union with Christ Jesus:

[2] May God our Father and the Lord Jesus Christ give you grace and peace.

[3] Let us give thanks to the God and Father of our Lord Jesus Christ! For in our union with Christ he has blessed us by giving us every spiritual blessing in the heavenly world. [4] Even before the world was made, God had already chosen us to be his through our union with Christ, so that we would be holy and without fault before him.

Because of his love [5] God had already decided that through Jesus Christ he would make us his sons and daughters – this was his pleasure and purpose. [6] Let us praise God for his glorious grace, for the free gift he gave us in his dear Son! [7] For by the blood of Christ we are set free, that is, our sins are forgiven. How great is the grace of God, [8] which he gave to us in such large measure!

In all his wisdom and insight [9] God did what he had purposed, and made known to us the secret plan he had already decided to complete by means of Christ. [10] This plan, which God will complete when the time is right, is to bring all creation together, everything in heaven and on earth, with Christ as head.

11 All things are done according to God's plan and decision; and God chose us to be his own people in union with Christ because of his own purpose, based on what he had decided from the very beginning. 12 Let us, then, who were the first to hope in Christ, praise God's glory!

13 And you also became God's people when you heard the true message, the Good News that brought you salvation. You believed in Christ, and God put his stamp of ownership on you by giving you the Holy Spirit he had promised. 14 The Spirit is the guarantee that we shall receive what God has promised his people, and this assures us that God will give complete freedom to those who are his. Let us praise his glory! *(Ephesians 1:1–14)*

In his letter to the church at Philippi, Paul says, 'Don't worry about anything, but in all your prayers ask God for what you need, always asking him with a thankful heart' (Phil 4:6). True to his own advice, Paul preludes his inter-cessions for the Ephesians with this chorale-like paean of praise. This exhortation to praise, which has been aptly called 'a great benediction', helps to focus our eyes on God (Eph 1:3,6,12,14).

We all, at some time in our lives, have experiences that stir and excite us, fire our imaginations and send us into a wonderland of dreams. For some, it may be the joy of receiving an unexpected gift, kindling within us feelings of mystery, tenderness and the assurance that we are loved. For others, quite different experiences produce a similar sense of wonder. Standing on a mountain-top in pristine snow, feet hidden in the glistening white, a keen breeze burning our cheeks, the air mildly stinging our lungs with fresh vitality, our eyes gazing across to even grander peaks and upward into a startling azure sky, then drifting downward into the green valleys far below.

We may find ourselves stirred by music, enthralled by some delicate painting, or intrigued by an intricate piece of engineering. Whatever it is that captures our being, we will find its equivalent in this glorious passage. For here is panorama and detail, here is the world of science and art; here the mind and the emotions meet. So I hope you will let yourself respond now as we scan Paul's grand vision of the God to whom we pray and take in some of the highlights along the way.

God has a plan

This is Paul's foundational concept. God has a plan and it is a plan for the cosmos; nothing is untouched by this plan, no matter how far we gaze into space. In all its vastness and intricacy, the whole universe will serve his glorious purpose. Each galaxy, every atom is designed to enhance the wonder and majesty of Jesus Christ (v 10).

Not only is this a promise for far-flung galaxies; it is a promise for our world, too. Every twist and turn of history, with its perplexing ambiguities, will lie unravelled at the feet of Christ. Every agony and ecstasy will one day find peace within the reflected light of his suffering love. Like a powerful magnet, Jesus will realign the random iron filings of all life, which at the moment lie in a state of confusion, into a pattern of beauty and meaning.

God has a plan for us too

Although God's eyes and hands can hold all time and space, he cares for each one of us personally. He has a purpose for each of us (Eph 1:5,11).

   [1] LORD, you have examined me and you know me.
   [2] You know everything I do;
      from far away you understand all my thoughts.
   [3] You see me, whether I am working or resting;

you know all my actions.
⁴ Even before I speak,
   you already know what I will say.
⁵ You are all round me on every side;
   you protect me with your power.
⁶ Your knowledge of me is too deep;
   it is beyond my understanding.
(Psalm 139:1–6)

It is mind-blowing to attempt to grasp all this, but it is true. The joy of it all is that God's plan is not to mash everything together like a pulp factory turning the colourful variety of waste paper – magazines, cartons, pictures and print – into some grey, uniform mass. No, God is the skilled creator, who from a mere hundred different atoms creates millions of different realities. Hence, in his great plan each will be released into their full, differentiated, enhanced potential. We, in the fullness of our personal individuality, are part of God's plan.

God has revealed this plan to us

The amazing truth does not stop there. God chooses to share his dream with us! What no human mind could dare to imagine, what no human intellect could hope to fathom, God has chosen to reveal. If God had not chosen to reveal it, we could never have known it. But with the insight he gives us, we can begin to grasp a little of the meaning behind creation and our place in it.

God's plan is a consequence of God's love. What motivates him is his desire for intimacy with us, his love, concern and compassion for us. There are no hidden agenda. We may ask, 'Why does God love us?' 'He loves us, because he loves us, because he loves us' – this was, I think, the conclusion to which the great Methodist preacher, Dr Sangster, came. But God's love is bigger than us. It is 'because of his love', not 'because of his love *for us*'. While we may each experience something of his love personally, and of his love for the human race focused supremely in Jesus, this is not the limit of his love. God loves the whole universe. Such a wide, all-embracing love has enormous consequences. These consequences are the direct out-working of his love in his relationship to us.

So he chooses us to be his. This is our destiny, this is our heart's throb. It is not something imposed on us like a giant's thumb pressing down on us; it is no alien force sucking us into a strange universe. This is what we are essentially made for – fellowship with God. We are not here only to 'till the soil', struggle with the elements, wrestle with our environment, or fight for survival. We are not here for God's amusement, for him to watch us, taunt-ing us with the knowledge that, strive as we might, we will always fail. Our highest purpose is not even to rule the world on his behalf! No, God made us for himself. He wants us to be whole and free. We are made for intimate relationship with him – to be neither his slaves nor his servants, but his children. He longs to be our Father and to share the intimacy of that trusting relationship.

He has also chosen us 'so that we would be holy and without fault before him' (Eph 1:4). Holiness is primarily a gift, not a daunting imposition. Because of who God is, we are to be holy as he is holy: 'he has created us for a life of good deeds, which he has already prepared for us to do' (2:10). Filled with his Spirit, we are called to a life of love and integrity; where destructive emotions cannot rot our hearts; where the words that flow from our lips are positive and praiseful; where relationships are constant, respectful and creative. Living such a life and reflecting God's character is only claiming our destiny. We are a new creation and we must 'put on the new self, which is creat-ed in God's likeness and reveals itself in the true life that is upright and holy' (4:24). This is God's purpose for us, this is our glorious future – to be a people destined for royalty, not the rubbish heap. What a glorious God!

But there is still more. As his people, God calls us to

hope in Christ (1:11–12). We are not to live in a fog of vague 'maybes'; rather, we are drawn on by magnetic certainty, upward with glowing hearts, onward by the power of love. Our hope is certain because God underwrites all his promises with his Holy Spirit – 'this assures us that God will give complete freedom to those who are his' (v 14). Freedom from self-centredness; freedom from sin; freedom from physical, emotional, relational and spiritual limitations. Freedom to be our true selves. Let us indeed praise his glory!

Already there is enough here to release a fountain of praise within us, endlessly rising and falling, touching our inner being with its refreshing music. But the greatest reason for praise is not the cause nor even the consequence of God's plan in our lives; it is the price he has willingly paid. Suddenly our value, our sense of self-worth soars immeasurably. Paul shares this stunning truth with us gradually, moving with deliberate hesitation to unfold his secret. Like a composer who knows he has a marvellously mind-stretching, heart-turning phrase to give us, he first hints at it, allowing us a brief glimpse, then a chance to catch our breath before he releases it to us in its full, haunting richness. Thus he leads us to the enormity of the cost to God of his plan – a cost vaster than the universe itself, 'the free gift he gave us in his dear Son' (v 6). Finally, the awesome truth is laid before us. Our freedom meant Christ's death: 'For by the blood of Christ we are set free, that is, our sins are forgiven. How great is the grace of God, which he gave to us in such large measure!' (vs 7–8).

> As we search the Word of God, we discover more and more of the riches we have in Christ. These riches were planned by the Father, purchased by the Son, and presented by the Spirit. *(Warren Wiersbe)* [2]

How do we respond to such a plan? Such love calls out from us a free-flowing response. 'Love so amazing, so divine, demands my life, my soul, my all.' But first we need to hear it (v 13) and be set free from our self-limitations. We also need to hear it over and over again. We can never hear it enough.

My wife, Eileen, has been a fine Christian for many years, coping with problems of bereavement, bringing up a family and supporting an over-committed minister for a husband. Yet a couple of years ago she heard again this plan of God's love in a new, life-giving way. It was God's word through Jeremiah which proved to be the key that unlocked a door that was closed on some area of darkness within her: 'I have loved you with an everlasting love; I have drawn you with loving-kindness' (Jer 31:3, *New International Version*). What a comfort! God will go on loving us for ever. We can never wear out his love, and nothing can separate us from it. These are all great truths which we need to hear, but this was not what spoke into Eileen's shadowland. Rather, it was the realisation that if God loves everlastingly, then *he has always loved her.* As she looked back on her childhood, to the times when she had felt unloved, she now knew that this was never the case: God was loving her then, too. 'In the name of our Lord Jesus Christ, always give thanks for everything to God the Father' (Eph 5:20). 'Always ... for everything.' How much more, now that we know God has loved us since before the world was made!

As we allow the Holy Spirit to instil in us – our minds, our emotions, our spirits and our bodies – this amazing truth of God loving us, we can receive it with gratitude: 'Let us, then, who were the first to hope in Christ, praise God's glory!' (1:12). These words focus on God himself rather than on what he has done. It is as though we had wiped the steamed-up mirror dry and seen him more vividly: 'Let us praise his glory!' (v 14).

How will we do this? Here are some suggestions for us to try. Some are for those working through this book on their own; some will work better in groups – these ideas can be adapted to suit either context. Try those that appeal to you most – you can always come back later to the others.

Prayer ideas
Alone

1. Play some music – perhaps songs of worship, perhaps some other type of music – whatever helps to light up the depths within you. As you listen, let the dream of this God who loves you so much filter through you – your body as well as your spirit, your emotions as well as your mind. As Jesus washed the feet of his disciples (John 13:1–9), so God wants to wash the weary and damaged parts of your being with the reality of his love.

Now let your mind and emotions, even your body, flow as you focus on the wonder of being loved by such a God. Dare to utter words of thanksgiving – though silence too can be an amazing expression of praise. If you speak in tongues, you may want to use this gift, but don't rush into tongues too quickly – allow the praise to build up inside you.

2. Write a love-letter to God – or you could paint, or use some other medium that helps you be free to express what you feel. When you have finished, keep it – it may rekindle your praise another time, just as a photograph can release buried memories.

3. You may feel more comfortable using other people's words or pictures. Spend some time selecting material that you think would help you express praise to God. (An anthology of prayers or a hymn/song book would be a good place to search.) Keep a note of what you have chosen – you may find it helpful for another occasion.

Together

1. Singing worship songs together can be a wonderful vehicle for praise, but why not sing to one another? This

From plan to praise

could be a solo exercise, though most of us would probably feel more comfortable if three or four people sang
together to the rest of the group.

As you listen, allow yourself to be carried on the wave
of other people singing – rather like a shell or piece of
drift wood is carried along by the tide. Let yourself be
moved further up the beach of God's heart. In between the
songs, share with each other the thoughts that came to
mind as you listened to others praising this God who
loves you so much.

2. Why not invite members of the group to read from
scripture some of the great words of praise, eg Psalms 95,
113, 136, 145; Revelation 4:9–11. It can be a powerful
experience to read these together, perhaps standing or
kneeling as seems appropriate.

3. Invite people to say short, sentence-long prayers of
praise to God the Father, the Son and the Holy Spirit. It
will add value if the passage in Ephesians is borne in mind
as you pray.

4. One person calls out names ascribed to God and the
rest of the group responds with short statements of
praise, eg Creator, Shepherd, Comforter, Judge, The
Truth, Teacher, Father, Redeemer, Empowerer. (Don't be
restricted to this list – there are many more.)

Section 1
EPHESIANS 1:15–23

1 FROM PRAISE TO PRAYER

15 For this reason, ever since I heard of your faith in the Lord Jesus and your love for all God's people, 16 I have not stopped giving thanks to God for you. I remember you in my prayers and 17 ask the God of our Lord Jesus Christ, the glorious Father, to give you the Spirit, who will make you wise and reveal God to you, so that you will know him. 18 I ask that your minds may be opened to see his light, so that you will know what is the hope to which he has called you, how rich are the wonderful blessings he promises his people, 19 and how very great is his power at work in us who believe. This power working in us is the same as the mighty strength 20 which he used when he raised Christ from death and seated him at his right side in the heavenly world. 21 Christ rules there above all heavenly rulers, authorities, powers, and lords; he has a title superior to all titles of authority in this world and in the next. 22 God put all things under Christ's feet and gave him to the church as supreme Lord over all things. 23 The church is Christ's body, the completion of him who himself completes all things everywhere. *(Ephesians 1:15–23)*

It was a privilege to see Nelson Mandela walk free from the confinement of so many years – and to walk with such dignity, to speak with such generosity and forgiveness. How had he managed to maintain his integrity and humanity under such circumstances? It was a privilege to listen to Terry Waite and John McCarthy speak of their intolerable imprisonment as hostages in Lebanon. But how did they keep sane? Part of the answer is that they did not allow their minds to be confined by their circumstances, by the pressures they faced, the opposition and hatred.

The man who wrote Ephesians was also a man confined (3:1). We do not know whether Paul could see the stars from his prison cell in Rome, but we can glimpse the vastness of his vision. Imprisoned he may have been, but it seems he was free to roam the heavens. If such freedom is a consequence of developing a fuller prayer life, then that is a prize worth pursuing.

Before we look at the content of his prayer in these verses in Ephesians, it is worth pausing to consider Paul's motives for praying. Notice how he begins (1:15–16). For Paul, the reasons for praising God are motivation for him to pray. Here, I think, is a first clue to power in prayer. Paul prays with a heart in tune with the strength of God's purpose. Because Christ has saved the Ephesians, and his Spirit is the guarantee that they will receive what God has promised, Paul is fired up to pray for them. Prayer is always more effective when we are in tune with God. Whatever the focus of our prayers, it is good to ask ourselves how it fits with God's plan. We could call this our *perennial* motive for prayer.

There is also a *prophetic* motive for prayer. When God reveals his will through a specific scripture, or maybe even a prophetic word or vision, he is inviting us to pray it into existence. He is asking us to be involved with him in bringing it about – as Jesus prayed, 'may your Kingdom come, may your will be done on earth as it is in heaven' (Matt 6:10). Prophecy is not something we normally have the responsibility of bringing about by direct action, but it is our part to pray for it. So, when we know something is the special will of God, we should pray with conviction.

For many of us, a *personal relationship* will be the powerful motivating factor. We don't need to apologise for this – it is part of the wonderful way God has made us.

What draws us to someone? What is it that makes us interested in them? Is it their popularity, their dynamic personality, their achievements, their power? Or is it their need, their courage or their circumstances? All can play a part and be used to stir us to prayer, but it is worth noting that Paul's personal motives were somewhat different. What counts for him is their 'faith in the Lord Jesus' (Eph 1:15). There is no stronger bond for Christians than this. One of the everyday miracles for us is meeting a stranger, discovering that he or she is a Christian and sensing the connection. We don't even need to meet someone in person – our joint allegiance to Christ is enough.

When I hear someone's personal testimony, it draws me to them. When I see what God is doing in their lives, I want to pray. It doesn't always need to be a great success story either.

In the past I have been asked, on occasion, to visit people who were dying at our local hospice – always an awesome privilege. One time the dying person was himself a doctor – we'll call him Robert. As our relationship developed, I discovered that over the last thirty years Robert had wandered further and further away from God. A difficult marriage led him into wrong relationships and his integrity pushed him away from Christian fellowship. Before this period, he had had many international adventures. He told me of his experiences as a young man in the last days of the Second World War and afterwards. Robert had known God's amazing guidance and provision. He had known the thrill of being used by God to bring others to Christ. He had sometimes suffered for his faith.

Now Robert was dying of a brain tumour. As a doctor, he knew the course his illness would take. As he told me of his journey with God, his faith, which had dwindled during his mid-years, was rekindled. I knew that wherever life had taken him, even into apparent agnosticism, the reality of his faith in the Lord Jesus could not be snuffed out. How I prayed for him. How special our fellowship was. Struggles, defeats, doubts and problems can all play a part in our faith.

Just as personal relationships can motivate us to pray for others, many of us find that praying *with* others also helps. Hundreds have felt the benefits of prayer schemes such as prayer triplets,[3] or the telephone prayer networks set up in churches.[4] Motivation for prayer becomes irresistible when our motives join forces with the constant motive of God's great purposes.

Three of Paul's motives for prayer shine out in this passage:

Thanking

For Paul, prayer begins and ends with giving thanks – for God and his wonderful plan, and for God's people. Though he could not be with them, the Ephesians were real people to him; they were individuals with names, abilities, problems, likes and dislikes, difficult pasts and challenging futures.

It is important that we give thanks for Christians we know – for those we find awkward or difficult, as well as those who love us and whose company we enjoy – because each is God's gift to us. Paul Wallis tells the story of a man called Andrew who had recently become a Christian: 'He told me excitedly how his prayer life (which itself was something of an experiment) had been transformed by adopting a new, quite simple habit, that of saying thank you to God ... "it was a joyful discovery"...' even though Andrew was going through an anxious and sad time.[5]

Learning to imbue our prayers with thanksgiving will not only transform our prayer life but also our relationships: 'A lively consciousness of mercies received ... gives birth to gratitude' (St Francis de Sales). As we thank God, we will find that we come to appreciate the gifts (that is, our fellow Christians) as well as the Giver. Thanksgiving cleanses our hearts and tunes us into his will in a special way.

Thinking

Paul doesn't leap straight from thanks to a catalogue of requests. He doesn't come to God with a pre-printed shopping list of spiritual goodies complete with tick boxes. Instead, having given thanks for the Ephesians, he takes time to recall them and to ponder their needs (Eph 1:16). He sees them as special people. He lingers over them in his mind. He longs to be with them; he loves them; he savours them.

Praying for others is perhaps easier when we can actually be with them – listen to them, touch them, see their response. But this form of praying need not be limited to those we are with physically or whom we know well. We may hold relative strangers or people far from us before God and he can, through his Spirit, help us know how to pray for them. Because we are 'one in Christ', God can and does help us appreciate their deepest needs. Often when I am praying for someone, I find that he will give me a picture which, as I hold it before him in prayer, develops towards the outcome he desires. Such remembering – with one hand in God's – is itself prayer. Many people pray like this far more than they realise; others make such prayer harder than they need to, because they don't spend enough time on the process of remembering or offer the process to God. However, few things are more deeply satisfying than mentally bringing our friends to the Lord.

Asking

Paul then moves on to intercede for his Ephesian colleagues. He is not afraid to make some fairly amazing requests. He first prays that their 'minds may be opened' (v 18) or, as the NIV puts it, 'that the eyes of [their hearts] may be enlightened'. This is not, of course, that they will have minds so open they believe anything; rather, he desires that they will have minds so aligned with God that they will know him and 'see his light'. It is not merely a theoretical, intellectual knowledge that Paul has in view; he is praying that their *hearts* will be opened, that their willed emotions will be fully responsive to the reality of God.

There is always more to discover about God. In any relationship, we will find that as we grow ever closer to another person we learn more about ourselves. As we grow in self-understanding, we learn more about the other. This is not a circular process but a spiral one! However, if we close our minds to others, we limit their freedom to interact with us. Then we close down the breadth and particularly the depth at which we can know them. How much more is this true of our relationship with God. He is far beyond our understanding, but the process of seeking to know him brings spiritual maturity (Eph 4:13).

However, for it to proceed we need the Spirit's help (1 Cor 2:6–13). Before we knew Christ, we were 'spiritually dead' (Eph 2:1). The scriptures make clear that all human beings are sinners and have fallen short of God's standard. As such, our minds have been blinded (1 Cor 2:9). Even as believers we have many blind spots. Without the Spirit's help, we could not appreciate the wonderful truth of Christ. This process of 'unblinding' is an ongoing one, not just for ourselves but for the whole Body of Christ. The 'opening of our minds' is part of our sanctification.

The world in which we live is in a fallen state, too. We find it difficult to grow in our understanding of God's beautiful reality. We are continually bombarded by unhealthy influences – from advertising, from half truths in the media, from the distortions that life's experiences bring. Additionally, Satan is the arch-deceiver and delights in misleading God's children, thus robbing them of their full relationship with God. Our understanding of the great truths of the faith do not take root automatically. They need constant replenishing – through Bible study, through the Christian community of which we are a part, but most of all through our engagement with Christ by which we are transformed (Rom 12:2; 2 Cor 3:18). This is a spiritual process, needing spiritual weapons for its successful completion.

Paul craves this 'open-mindedness' so that the Ephesians would 'know what is the hope to which he has called [them]' (Eph 1:18). Christian hope is God's resource for us to overcome all the pressures of life (Rom 5:2–5). For us as Christians, our God-given hope is not something vague and uncertain; rather, it is guaranteed, based on God's promises and underwritten by his Spirit (Eph 1:13–14). Once we are gripped by God's hope, we are empowered; our perceptions, our desires and our attitudes are changed, and so is our freedom to act. Hope is a powerful motivator.

A fisherman is dependent on the tide before he can sail. Without it, his boat is high and dry, keeled over, stuck in the mud. Once he sees the signs that the tide has turned and the sea is beginning to flow back, he is filled with hope. He knows that in time the sea will return, his boat will float and he can set sail. In the same way, the Christian knows that there is no possibility of disappointment. But 'time and tide wait for no man'. We need to live alert to our hope so that we don't miss the tide.

Paul also wants the Ephesians to know 'how rich are the wonderful blessings he promises his people' (Eph 1:18). Christ died so that we could become God's inheritance. It may not seem like that to us, we may not appear as such to others, but God regards us as part of his great wealth – we are jewels in his crown, we are precious to him. If we are to develop as God wants us to, we need to know this truth deep within us.

I met Anna by the bedside of her slowly dying father. I came to know her well as we shared those intimate hours of waiting for death. Her mother was a manic-depressive; her father favoured her brother over her. When I discovered the powerful negative environment in which she had lived, I was puzzled as to how she had become such a gentle, quietly strong, balanced, outgoing, caring person. She should not be like that! One day she revealed the secret. As a child she had gone to a Brethren Assembly where she had met people who were loving and kind to her, in particular one couple whom she had come to call Auntie and Uncle. She would stay with Auntie and Uncle at weekends. 'They would spoil me terribly, and shower me with love.' In effect, they told her – by their words, by their hugs, by their attitudes, by their actions – that she mattered very much.

Whether unemployed or overworked, taken for granted by spouse or children, living alone and desperate for companionship, old, young or somewhere in between, we need to know that we are treasured by God and destined for his heavenly kingdom. This was true for the Christians in Ephesus; we know it is true today for ordinary people like ourselves.

Paul wants the Ephesians to know 'how very great is [God's] power at work in us who believe' (Eph 1:19–20). If this is not a reality for us, the promised hope will mock us and the blessings will seem beyond our reach. We need God's power in order to live as Christian people in the kind of alien culture which was the lot of the Ephesians and is still the case for most of us. 'If God's call looks back to the beginning and God's inheritance looks to the end, then surely God's 'power' spans the interim' (John Stott). Only God's power can see us through from the call to the glory. Paul gives us indisputable evidence for this, all of which is focused on Christ Jesus:

- His resurrection from the dead.

- His rule over all supernatural forces.

- His comprehensive supremacy throughout the universe.

God's power, which places Christ on the throne of the universe, began with what? A powerless, deserted man? No, worse – all God had to work with was the defeated, mutilated, dead body of Jesus. Whenever we are tempted to doubt God's power to change us, here is the antidote. But we need our minds and hearts open to know this truth. We need this light to penetrate the darkness of our despair. For Paul's point is that God's power is demonstrated not only in Christ but in the Christian, and not only its potential but its actuality. No wonder we, too, need to pray for minds that are open.

Prayer ideas
Alone

1. If you are alone by choice, begin by thanking God for the space and time he has given you. Then reflect on the aspects of your situation you appreciate most. Allow your recollections to turn towards God in thanksgiving.

2. If you have not chosen to be alone, but are so because of circumstances, thank God for the knowledge that Paul was also in enforced isolation. Thank God for Paul and for others you have heard about, who were used by God in their isolation – Jesus during his temptations, John Bunyan, Dietrich Bonhoeffer, Richard Wurmbrand and Terry Waite are some examples that come to my mind.

3. Make a list of some aspects of God and your journey with him that are special to you (you could start with the names attributed to him, see page 21, No. 4 'Together'). Then try to recall how you first discovered this truth about God and the times this knowledge has been valuable to you.

Alternatively, you could list episodes from the life of Jesus which you particularly value, then seek to identify what it is about God that these stories show you. Take some time over this, then thank God for his involvement in your life.

4. Whom do you know who would be blessed by living in the knowledge of God's truth as you are? Pray that their minds will be opened to God's light – be as specific as you can. For instance, you might pray for someone with Parkinson's disease who feels frustrated and powerless. You could pray for their healing. You could pray for the truth of God's power to fill them so that they can accept their weakness and come to know that, in eternity, they will be restored and transformed as Jesus was at the resurrection. Pray, too, that they will be helped to see how God can use them in their weakness. However, as you pray, be prepared for God to steer your mind towards new and unexpected ways of praying for them.

Together

1. Pair up with someone and share aspects of God that are special to you (you might wish to begin with No. 3 'Alone' above). Explain why each is special to you and invite your partner to comment on whether these aspects are important to them, how and why. Then reverse the process. Ask God to give you insights through one another.

2. In a small group (not more than four), talk about people who have meant a lot to you as you have grown as a Christian. You can either ask each other questions about them; or you could name the individuals you have remembered, then each sit quietly for five minutes or more, asking the Holy Spirit to bring to mind all that was enjoyable about your special person. Take time to pray for these people.

Finally, use another five minutes of quietness to ask the Holy Spirit to bring to mind Christians you have known but have forgotten to pray for recently. Give thanks for each. You may wish to promise God that you will go on praying for them.

3. Share with one another why it is you value others in the group. Then pray for each other, thanking God for the blessing he has provided through each of you.

2 PRAYER AND THE SPIRIT

> I remember you in my prayers and ask the God of
> our Lord Jesus Christ, the glorious Father, to give you
> the Spirit, who will make you wise and reveal God to
> you...
>   Pray on every occasion, as the Spirit leads.
> *(Ephesians 1:16–17; 6:18)*

There is an intimate connection between the work of the
Spirit and prayer. Prayer involves committing ourselves
to God's mind and joining our wills with his mighty purposes. The more we know of God, the more we are likely
to understand what his will is and to hear the Spirit's wise
guiding. As we hear the Spirit's wisdom, he reveals to us
God's will for specific situations which, in turn, motivates
us to pray with energised relevance.

The best prayer reflects back to God what he has
revealed to us of his will. This is what I would call 'surfboard praying'. Surfboarding has always looked scary to
me. Using a surfboard, the surfer seeks to stay on the
moving edge of the wave, carried along by its enormous
power. He doesn't need to struggle to move. Prayer can
be the same kind of experience. We don't need to struggle to pray. We only need to go with the flow, even when
it seems strange to us, asking the Spirit leads us to the
heart of a problem, whether it be personal, economic or

social. Often God chooses initially not to reveal the whole truth to us. But as we show our agreement with him and our willingness to pray in the way he is directing, the front edge of the prayer-wave carries us along.

Although there is an ease with this kind of praying, there is some work involved, too. We have to wait for the wave, stay alert, keep ourselves fit and the board ready for God's timing. Getting up speed is not always easy. Equally, we don't need to be too hard on ourselves – God loves us. Another wave will come. It doesn't even matter if we fall off. He will give us another opportunity to try again.

In his book *Love on its Knees*, Dick Eastman gives an account of his meeting with Mark Gippert.[6] In the spring of 1986, Mark was called by the Spirit to pray for a month in key cities in the USSR. His mission concluded with four days of prayer in Kiev. Mark went to the square in the centre of Kiev and sat down to pray under a huge statue of Lenin. Every fifteen minutes he changed the focus of his intercession for believers in Russia. He could tell when a fifteen-minute period had passed because a gigantic clock in the square let out a bong each quarter-hour.

On the last day, just before noon, Mark was suddenly convinced that God had heard his prayers and that even then something was happening – something that would shake the Soviet Union, something God would use to bring more freedom. But he needed confirmation of this, so he prayed, 'O God, give me a sign...' Just then, in the distance, the hands of the huge clock moved to the twelve o'clock position. Mark waited for twelve chimes. They never came. It was as though God was saying that the old pattern was over. The very next day Mark began hearing about Chernobyl.

Chernobyl was a terrible nuclear disaster with ongoing destructive effects, but it was also the beginning of the end of the Communist regime. *Glasnost* was forced on the Soviet Union: being secretive was not an option. Suddenly, whether they wanted to or not, they were forced to be open. At a General Conference for all party leaders (the first for forty-seven years), President Gorbachev announced sweeping changes – changes that would lead to the break-up of the USSR. 'When we stand before God ... we will learn that intercessory prayer has more to do with bringing about positive changes in our world than any other spiritual activity' (Eastman). This was not just intercessory prayer; it was prayer as God directed, led by his Spirit. Here are some of the ways in which the Spirit is essential for our praying.

The Holy Spirit reveals God to us

The Holy Spirit is the author of scripture. He helps us see the living God through the written word, and brings to our mind all we need to know of Christ. Furthermore, the Holy Spirit knows the mind of God in the same way that the spirit of a human being knows the mind of that person (1 Cor 2:11–12). The Spirit reveals all that can be known of God. He enables us to tune into God's own heart and share his expectations. The more we know of God, the better equipped we are to pray. The more we know of what God is seeking to accomplish in the world, the more we can co-operate with him. Our experience of prayer becomes rewarding.

The Holy Spirit makes us wise for prayer

Wisdom is knowledge applied. It is the understanding of God's character working itself out in myriad mundane circumstances. Wisdom is a valuable gift for any of us as we pray about real people, real situations and real needs.

John Wimber has contributed to thousands of people's understanding and experience of God's healing ministry. His own journey began with many months of study and preaching, during which he felt the Holy Spirit revealing to him God's desire to heal. God gave John experiences of healing and showed him how to apply and expand his knowledge in many contexts. John believed that the Holy Spirit was teaching him how to co-operate with the visible signs of what God was doing and to pray for 'more of the same'. This meant that if the Spirit was causing hurts to surface in a person, John didn't try to quell those hurts – which is the normal human response, especially if you have a pastoral nature. Rather, he asked God to continue drawing them out until release came. If a physical problem led to someone talking about a traumatic emotional problem, John would pray for the emotional issue. The Holy Spirit taught John how to apply his God-given insight in personal ministry and how to transfer this insight to others so that they, too, could be used in God's healing ministry.

> But if any of you lack wisdom, you should pray to
> God, who will give it to you; because God gives
> generously and graciously to all. *(James 1:5)*

The Holy Spirit guarantees God's promises

I am not at all in favour of the Lottery scratch cards, but the way they work is that people buy a card and scratch the numbers to see if they have the winning combination. If so, they can claim the prize there and then. This kind of 'instant satisfaction' is the opposite to prayer. Prayer is not meant to be a quick fix. We do sometimes get crisp, clear, prompt answers – and when these come, they are valuable not only in themselves but because of the positive imprint they leave on our spirits that God does indeed answer prayer. However, expecting 'instant satisfaction' is not helpful. It encourages us to think that because there is no visible answer, 'God has not heard'. Prayer is more like a long-term investment in an insurance policy. We need to keep on praying. While the emphasis and direction of our prayer for a person or situation will change, our commitment will not.

But we need inner encouragement, and this is where the Holy Spirit impinges on prayer yet again: 'The Spirit is the guarantee that we shall receive what God has promised his people...' (Ephesians 1:14).

Sometimes the view is presented that if we were better Christians – if all our relationships were right, all our sins were not only confessed and forgiven but left behind us, and we had sufficient of the right kind of faith – then all our prayers would be answered more quickly and more clearly. The fog of confusion as to whether God had said 'Yes', 'No', 'Wait', 'Pray again', 'Stop', 'Go', would not be our experience! Most of us sigh inwardly: 'If only...'

Even Jesus, the Son of God, knew that there are times when, for whatever reason, we need to keep pestering God (Luke 18:1–8). However, at such times we need not be driven by fear of failure or by desperation. Instead, we should allow ourselves to be carried along by the mighty wave of God's Spirit. It is he who assures us of God's concern, power, and love. It is he who provides us with the evidence that God will do what he has promised. He is the guarantee that God will do all that he commits himself to do.

It is a special aspect of the Spirit's guaranteeing work, perhaps the supreme aspect of his ministry, that we are 'able to come in the one Spirit into the presence of the Father' (Eph 2:18). A few years ago, I was due to speak at a church in America. Although I had only been in the States just over a day, on the Saturday morning I joined a small group of people who were committed to praying for their fellowship. Even though I was a stranger, I felt very much at home with these few folk in prayer. We knew that we stood as one before the same God, who was our Father even though we were from different continents and traditions.

As we prayed, one of the insights the Spirit made clear to us was that many in their church were standing outside this place of intimacy. They did not quite believe that God wanted them to step into his presence. It seemed as though the door was open but they dare not quite go in – though they wanted to. This picture was not in any way condemning. Indeed, as we reflected on it, God gave us all an intense longing that others should know his love for them as individuals, and enjoy the awesome freedom of the children of God:

> 14 Those who are led by God's Spirit are God's children. 15 For the Spirit that God has given you does not make you slaves and cause you to be afraid; instead, the Spirit makes you God's children, and by the Spirit's power we cry out to God, 'Father! my Father!' 16 God's Spirit joins himself to our spirits to declare that we are God's children. 17 Since we are his children, we will possess the blessings he keeps for his people, and we will also possess with Christ what God has kept for him; for if we share Christ's suffering, we will also share his glory. *(Romans 8:14–17)*

We need the Holy Spirit to minister within us before we can pray, 'Father! my Father!' When we can pray this – understanding its full implications, and freed by the Spirit to become the children that we are – then we will hear God, love God, obey God and pray aright. As we approach that quality of relationship, the Holy Spirit will remind us of the things in our lives that we need to sort out, where we need to be forgiven, where we need to offer forgiveness, where we need to be fathered.

There can and should be a deep level of intimacy in our prayers. Intimacy is not at all the same thing as informality, casualness or plain laziness. Intimacy is costly. We have to be willing to be totally open and to share in the pain and the desires of the other. Intimacy tenders to the other the utmost respect. God is the one with whom, through his Spirit, we can become most intimate. This intimacy is inextricably linked to a deep trust of him as our Father, in whose presence we can be utterly ourselves. We may need the Spirit's healing to grow into intimacy and we will consider this further later. But with intimacy comes power in prayer. This is certainly part of what it means to pray in the Spirit.

Praying in freedom

> 23 'But the time is coming and is already here, when by the power of God's Spirit people will worship the Father as he really is, offering him the true worship that he wants. 24 God is Spirit, and only by the power of his Spirit can people worship him as he really is.'
> (John 4:23–24)

We are living in the time that 'is coming and is already here' – the era of the Spirit. Prayer is not restricted to a church building – anywhere will do. This is our freedom 'in the Spirit'. It does not preclude us having a personal place for prayer, such as a particular desk or room, nor is it to deny the value of a public place dedicated to worship. I get a tremendous sense of God's presence in a great parish church, with its strong pillars and vaulted roof, even though it cuts across my theology! But we should not be dependent on or restricted to that place. We are free to pray 'in the Spirit' on the train, in the car, at work...

Praying in scripture

Praying in the Spirit is not just about release from restrictions. We need to pray in conformity with 'the word of God ... the sword which the Spirit gives you' (Eph 6:17). Scripture can be both a positive vehicle for prayer and a means of helping us grow in prayer.

Prayer is so clearly God's business, we should be keen to discover 'the values' by which his business operates. Scripture reveals these principles to us. Here are four to consider.

Righteousness is a fundamental value for God, so it should be no surprise that 'The prayer of a good person has a powerful effect' (James 5:16). Our sin cuts us off from God. Even as forgiven Christians, children of God with a perpetual right to come to the centre of power in the universe, our sin will hinder us. So what must happen?

> If we confess our sins to God, he will keep his promise and do what is right: he will forgive us our sins and purify us from all our wrongdoing. *(1 John 1:9)*

Awareness of our sin need not exclude us from powerful prayer. Rather, the desire to be powerful in prayer drives us to confession and cleansing.

Closely allied to righteousness is *obedience*. Without an obedient heart, we will be out of touch with God. Jesus promises the converse of this: if we obey his word, we remain in his love; if we remain in him and his word remains in us, we can ask for anything we wish and have it (John 15:5–10).

Faith is another fundamental principle for prayer: 'No one can please God without faith, for whoever comes to God must have faith that God exists and rewards those who seek him' (Heb 11:6). One of our difficulties here is distinguishing between faith as positive feelings and faith as trust in God. Faith operates on what we know of God and of his will. Our asking for certain things may 'feel' ridiculous or hopeless, but if we are sure that it is from God, let us ask with confidence in him (James 1:6).

Finally, we need to *pray in Jesus' name*: coming to God through Christ and not trusting in our own righteousness; praying only for what accords with his will; praying in love and fellowship with his people; knowing who God is through Jesus; and praying in the strength of Christ's childlike trust in his Father.

The Bible is full of God's promises to his people. Such promises show us the heart of God, his way of doing things in given situations, his response to needs. When we pray, we can hold up to him the promises of scripture and direct our prayers with a deep confidence that we are on the right track. This is not an automatic guarantee of success, and God's promises should not be taken out of context. Rather, we must understand their circumstances and see them as signposts that lead us to God. (Some of the promises of God which I find useful to keep in mind as I pray are included in the 'Ideas' section at the end of this chapter, 'Alone', No. 3.)

Another way we can allow the Spirit to lead us to pray with scripture is to plead as the people of God. What I mean by this is that we stimulate our praying by using the words of God's people in scripture. Here are some examples from the psalms:

> I am worn out, O LORD; have pity on me!
>   Give me strength...
> *(Psalm 6:2)*

> 1 God, be merciful to us and bless us;
>   look on us with kindness,
> 2 so that the whole world may know your will;
>   so that all nations may know your salvation.
> *(Psalm 67:1–2)*

> 5 My sins, O God, are not hidden from you;
>   you know how foolish I have been...
> 6 Don't let me bring disgrace to those
>   who worship you,
>   O God of Israel!
> *(Psalm 69:5–6)*

These verses could be used as patterns for prayer or they could be spoken as prayers. God's people have prayed the psalms throughout generations and, like a mature wine or a piece of well-seasoned timber, they bring richness and depth. The emotions and situations depicted in them often provide a good route to praying about our own feelings and circumstances.

Praying in tongues

Praying in the Spirit properly includes praying in tongues.[7] When we don't know what to ask for or even how to pray, the Spirit comes to our aid:

> [26] ...the Spirit himself pleads with God for us in groans that words cannot express. [27] And God, who sees into our hearts, knows what the thought of the Spirit is; because the Spirit pleads with God on behalf of his people and in accordance with his will.
> *(Romans 8:26–27)*

These 'groans that words cannot express', which reach the surface of our being and become audible, may be unintelligible to others, but they are a language God understands. I would want to emphasise, however, that such prayer is God helping us, not God putting us under yet another burden of failure because we don't/can't/won't pray in tongues. Neither is there any justification for any sense of superiority in being able to pray in tongues. Our tears, our pain, our cries of anguish, our inexpressible thoughts can be the Spirit praying in us just as much our speaking in tongues.

When we cannot express our prayers, God can still receive us as praying people. He is not dependent on our being articulate or knowing the correct grammar or the 'right' words. Indeed, if we rely too much on these, our prayers are in danger of becoming a performance rather than genuine prayer. However, praying in tongues is no cheap option. It expresses what is too much for human minds and hearts to hold. Indeed, such language reaches beyond words to a deeper level than the intellect.

Praying in community

> 'Again, I tell you that if two of you on earth agree about anything you ask for, it will be done for you by my Father in heaven.' *(Matthew 18:19, NIV)*

Prayer is not meant to be always a solitary struggle. A praying community can offer each other support and encouragement, and sustain each other for far longer than a lone individual. On a long flight, a flock of geese will adopt the aerodynamic 'V' formation. The leader takes the strain of wind resistance, while the others encourage the front flyer by 'honking'. Eventually, when the leader tires, another bird takes over. In this way they cover vast distances and manage to maintain their homeward direction.

There are many potential relationships that can develop into prayer fellowships. There are the bonds of family, of common interests, of belonging to the same church. There are Christian friends with whom we have a comfortable, positive relationship. In all these relationships, we need to take the risk of venturing out in prayer together. If we don't, we may lose the opportunity for the bond of fellowship to grow to even greater depth. A friend with whom I discussed this issue commented, 'Never have I pushed past that awkward moment into prayer with the other and regretted it. More often than not I have been thrilled at the outcome or resulting fellowship in prayer.'

Clearly we are unlikely to end up praying together without taking some action. Why not take the initiative and simply invite a couple of friends to meet to pray together? This will show them how much you value their friendship and their support as Christians. Praying together could well enhance your relationship and build your faith. There will also be the opportunity to dare to try new ways of praying, which people often find safer in a small group; for example, praying out loud, or working through a meditation together.

A specific, personal need, which you or someone else may have, often serves as an impetus to bring people together to pray. Care needs to be taken here to ensure that no confidences are broken. When the immediate problem is resolved, the prayer fellowship could continue as praying becomes an integral part of their life together.

Alternatively, two or more people could form a prayer triplet or a prayer pair which is committed to praying for an external organisation or issue, such as a local school, a neighbourhood, or a local or national problem.

And finally, a challenge: perhaps you could take the risk of praying with someone with whom you sense some kind of natural barrier or relational resistance. The Spirit can then use the experience of praying to lead you both towards a positive, quality relationship.

Prayer ideas
Alone

1. Set aside time to listen to God. Ask him to guide you as to what you should pray for and how you should pray. Spend fifteen minutes or so focusing on God, perhaps by reading a psalm; then be quiet. At the end of the time, write down some of the ideas and mental pictures you have had. They probably won't seem like great 'visions from God'. Nevertheless, simply start to use them as a focus for your praying and allow your prayer to flow (aloud or silently). Please don't be anxious if progress is slow.

2. If you want to pray 'in tongues' but don't do so at the moment, why not meet with someone who already has experience in this way of praying? Share your feelings and fears, and listen to what your friend has to say. Both of you can pray that God will enable you to use this gift of his Spirit. Sometimes people can recognise the 'thought patterns in tongues' before expressing them. There is no need to panic if nothing happens; God will give you further opportunities for growth, so keep seeking. He may show you other aspects of prayer or other issues you may need to work through first. Speaking in tongues is not a 'step up the spiritual ladder' nor does it make us more acceptable to God. He already loves us totally.

3. Here are some of God's promises to us, which you may want to use as a starting point for prayer:

- Wisdom, James 1:5.

- A way out of an impossible situation, 1 Corinthians 10:13.

- Our needs met, Matthew 6:31–33; Psalm 37:3.

- God's comforting presence in trouble, Isaiah 43:1–2.

- God's ability to bring good out of difficult, dangerous or evil circumstances, Romans 8:28.

- God's love which is stronger than any negative force, Romans 8:37–39.

- God's light for our darkness, John 12:46.

Write some of these verses in a column down one side of a sheet of paper. Then, opposite these, note down any situations that need God to act in the way the verse is describing. Pray the verses, applying them to the situations. Praying the scriptures like this often helps to increase and maintain our faith under pressure. In fact, learning to pray like this can add a new sense of excitement to our study of scripture. You may find it helpful to keep a record of the promises of God you discover. Alternatively, many situations are covered by the verses listed at the front of the Gideons Bible.

It is also good to memorise key verses, which the Holy Spirit can bring to mind when we need them.

Together

1. Perhaps finding a special place or time to pray will help you. Alternatively, you could try praying anywhere and everywhere. Invite a friend to do this with you. Agree when you will start, discuss how you think it might work, and commit yourselves to praying for one another as you set out on your journey together. Maybe share your apprehensions and hopes. Use your prayer times to share your experiences, give thanks to God for the good ones, encourage each other in the difficult ones – and laugh together too!

2. In a group, hold hands in a relaxed way and then pray for the person on your left. Ask the Spirit to fill you with love for that person. Let your God-given love flow towards them. Invite the Spirit to help you pray for them by bringing things to your mind and heart. If nothing does, don't be anxious. Instead, try to relax and think lovingly and positively about the person, simply asking God to bless them. After praying for the person on your left, do the same for the person on your right.

After a few minutes, ask the group if any of them would welcome specific prayer. If so, everyone can focus their prayers on the individuals they are praying for, perhaps laying hands on them gently.

3. Ask the group to share promises of scripture which have helped them, particularly those that have helped them to pray during difficult situations.

4. Consider together some situations described in the Bible and how they might show you what to pray for in some current situations. These could be personal, church, local community or national.

3 **PRAYER AND HOPE**

> 18 I ask that your minds may be opened to see his
> light, so that you will know what is the hope to
> which he has called you, how rich are the wonderful
> blessings he promises his people, 19 and how very
> great is his power at work in us who believe.
> *(Ephesians 1:18–19)*

Through the Spirit, our minds are opened to see God's
light. As God's light dawns in us, so hope is born. This is
more than normal human hoping: it is God-given hope
and, though it is not yet our present experience, it is
secure enough to build a life on.

But why should we link prayer with hope? Because to
pray effectively, Christians need to know God's hope.
Hope is part of the Christian's life-support system. If we
have hope, we can live appropriately for Christ (Eph 4:1 –
6:9). We can see this at work when Paul reached Philippi.

When Paul came to Philippi, he knew he was called by
God to be there (Acts 16:10–12). He had had quite a struggle arriving at this knowledge. Perhaps one of the reasons
God had kept him searching was so that when he got
there he would be absolutely sure he was meant to be
there, for trouble was soon to come and his certainty
would be severely tested. He ended up in prison with his
companion, Silas – in the stocks, their backs bleeding

from a severe beating. But they did not think, 'This is it then – the end of the road. See what a mess God has got us into!' There in prison, 'Paul and Silas were praying and singing hymns to God' (Acts 16:25).

Note, however, that it wasn't only their singing that caused the earthquake which would free them! It was their praying. What helped them to pray in such circumstances? Paul and Silas knew hope. This is not simply a matter of them feeling naturally optimistic – their physical state was certainly not conducive to that kind of feeling! Rather, they could pray because they knew that God wanted them in Philippi. They may or may not have known that God wanted them out of prison, but they were sure he had sent them there for the progress of the gospel.

We can see how such hope can work in practice if we reflect on the way John Wimber's healing ministry developed. Wimber taught that Christians should pray in hope. To heal the sick is part of our Christian calling; to believe that God can and wants to heal the sick is part of our Christian hope. It is not just wishful thinking; it is part of the truth of the gospel. So we can and should pray for healing, and persevere in praying for it. Until Wimber explained and modelled these truths, many Christians prayed for healing without any sense of expectation. But when God's hope was established in their minds and hearts, they discovered they could pray differently and often with different results.

Some of Jesus' teaching underlines this necessity to pray in hope, that is, to pray on the basis of things which, though unseen, are sure because they are guaranteed by God. Looking at the parable of the widow and the judge (Luke 18:1–8), the widow persisted because she sensed that justice must be done (v 3). Her hope was her motivating factor. In the similar parable of the friends at midnight, it is his hope that his friend would honour the rules of hospitality and the bonds of friendship which motivates the first man to pester the second (11:5–8). And sometimes before answers to prayer can come there are spiritual struggles to go through which require time and endurance on our part. Daniel discovered this when he prayed and fasted for three weeks before he had his vision of an angel by the River Tigris (Dan 10:2–14).

A clear grasp of the hope to which God calls us is certain to help us in our prayers. Christian hope is valid; it is not pie in the sky when you die. Christian hope is based on the unfailing promises of God. So let's survey some of those promises and see how they can help us pray with confidence and commitment, seizing hold of our God-given hope and not letting anything or anyone take it from us:

- *Romans 8:17:* 'Since we are his children, we will possess the blessings he keeps for his people, and we will also possess with Christ what God has kept for him...'

- *Romans 8:21:* A promise for all creation – 'creation itself would one day be set free from its slavery to decay and would share the glorious freedom of the children of God'.

- 2 *Corinthians 5:1–5:* We are promised a new and glorious resurrection body when we die – a body which is, qualitatively, as much superior to our present one, even in its prime, as a well-built mansion is superior to a tent. A tent is a very serviceable shelter for campers, but we can look forward to our mansion!

- *Philippians 3:8–11:* We will share life fully with Christ.

- *Philippians 2:10–11:* A promise for unbelievers – 'all beings in heaven, on earth, and in the world below will fall on their knees, and all will openly proclaim that Jesus Christ is Lord'.

- *1 John 3:2–3:* we will become like Christ.

It is important not to give up on hope or prayer when we don't see immediate results. So often we grow weary when we pray for a situation and see no change, let alone a crisp, unambiguous answer. At these times, it is a great help to have others praying with us, to offer encouragement, support and prayer in fellowship, and to hold up to one another the promises of God.

In the early twentieth century, James Frazer was called to pray for the people of Lisu in China. He prayed for them for many years without any apparent 'success', but he kept on and on witnessing and praying because he had a God-given hope. Eventually his prayers were answered, as though the rain had cleared and the sun shone brightly through the clouds. Large numbers of people came to a living faith in Jesus, and their lives were transformed.

We may have similar hopes and dreams for ourselves, our families, our churches, our friends. They may seem to come from nowhere, borne on an ocean current of love. They may ebb and flow, returning to our consciousness many times before they take shape. When we long for our neighbours to know Jesus Christ, when we dream of using our gifts for Christ, we can pray these thoughts back to God, asking him to bring them about. Then we can seek to understand what the next step might be and pray for that, too. The desires of our hearts, when those hearts are cleansed by the Holy Spirit, will be echoes of God's desires. The results we are longing for will often have his seal of approval.

Of course, there are risks. We need to bring our dreams to the judgement seat of Christ and allow him to sift them to see if they are his desire. Many things we will immediately recognize as not being from Christ. We need to be willing to let the Holy Spirit do his work of dredging our subconscious. Jamie Buckingham gives a graphic account of this process in his own life:[8]

> Miss Carver, who was in her mid-eighties, was
> speaking about the gentle ways God uses to mould

us until we begin to look like Jesus Christ. The more I listened, the more painful it became. It was as though God was attacking the cancer sores in my inner nature with a sharp scalpel, scraping and cutting out the infection.

Jamie soon discovered that there were yet deeper levels of his subconscious which needed cleansing and healing. Later, he went to a trusted friend to ask him why, after sharing with his wife 'events which I had for years pushed beneath the surface of my lake in a vain attempt to keep them hidden', he had relived many of his carnal activities in his dreams:

> [His friend] smiled and said, 'The Holy Spirit is busy dredging up the junk in your subconscious, letting it float to the surface.' 'But what can I do with it?' I asked. 'Rebuke it! When you rebuke these memories of the past you not only cast them out, but you close the door on the areas where they first came in.'

Such a process is often deeply painful, but as God carries out this process of purification, so the dreams of our hearts will more and more correspond with his hopes.

Here are some safeguards we should apply to ensure that our hopes are in line with God's hopes:

- We can invite a trusted Christian friend to check them out.

- We can measure them against scriptural insight.

- We can adopt Gamaliel's attitude (Acts 5:33–39) that God would allow them to grow or die, depending on whether or not they are in his will. This is a difficult tightrope to balance on, because when a dream fades, how can we know that it is God removing our desires, and not simply our lethargy? If a hope remains or develops, how do we know whether it is God maintaining our hope and not our stubbornness clinging to it? But we can trust God to sort out our problems if we are seeking to walk by the Spirit. We are not so complex or so unusual that God cannot handle us!

Perhaps my own experience will help to show how all of this can work out in practice, as well as offer some comfort if you are going through a time of self-questioning.

A few years ago, as I was praying, I was surprised by a thought that seemed to come out of nowhere: 'What do you want to do with the rest of your life, David?' My first response was to dismiss it, but something made me think this could be God addressing me. So, over the next couple of days, I tried to answer the question as honestly as I could. In the end I concluded, 'I most want to enable as many people as possible, to lead as many other people to Christ as is possible.' Not a very neat piece of English! But the sense of significance and hope meant that I prayed my dream. Soon afterwards a denominational post with a national responsibility was advertised. It seemed as though it was the open door to fulfil this God-given desire about which I had prayed. In the end, however, it came to nothing. Had I misheard God?

I could well have gone on a guilt trip at this point, but I didn't. I knew God loved me even if it were my misguided self leading me the wrong way. And anyway he would approve of my wanting others to come to Christ. Neither did I panic and rush around grabbing any and every opportunity to move to a new job. Rather, I committed myself to apply that 'desire of my heart' to my present circumstances. I confirmed this with sensitive and trusted Christian friends who knew me well. I believed that it came from God and that I could leave its fulfilment to him.

Sometimes the desire would surface and my hopes would quicken. I persevered in praying for their fulfilment. I was also working towards my goal in my church situation and wider afield. Sometimes when things were not moving as quickly and fully as I would like in the direction of that hope, I would feel pain over what I sensed was our failure – mine especially as leader. But overall I felt at 'peace with God'.

About two years later I was putting the *Baptist Times* in the bin, when my wife checked me with these words: 'Have you seen the advert for the post at the Evangelical Alliance? It seems to be just the job you are looking for.' I persisted in my intention of placing the paper in the bin, but she was somehow more insistent. So I looked, prayed, applied and was appointed. It sounds so easy put like that, but such a brief sentence covers many months of prayer, of waiting, of interviews, of heart-searching and pain for myself and for the church I had pastored for twelve years – a time when God was preparing us to fulfil the hope of my calling.

On reflection, how crucial it was that I had owned up to the hope within me; that I had taken the risk of following through on that hope by praying; that I had shared it with others; and that God had given me the grace to walk in the path he had laid out. It is good for us, individually, as a family, as a group within a church or as a whole church, to dream our dreams. It is important that, like Paul, we pray for one another to know the hopes to which we are called, and that we support one another prayerfully in those hopes.

George Bernard Shaw said, 'You see things and you say "why?" but I dream things that never were and I say "why not?!" ' How much more do we need to dream for God and ask him, 'Why not?' That is why he gives us hope!

Prayer ideas
Alone

It is particularly important that we make time and space to dream. By space, I mean not primarily physical solitude – although that may help – but freedom from the demands of daily pressures. You may find it helpful to go on a retreat or a walk, or you may be able to create space in the anonymity of a long car journey, or on the bus or tube.

1. Dream dreams for God and with God. What excites you in the Christian field? What causes you pain when it is not being carried through? Share your hopes and concerns with God.

2. Many of us will have dismissed the hopes God has given us along our faith journey. Without getting bogged down in guilt, you may want to say sorry to God if you have too quickly rejected his thoughts. Ask him to bring them back to mind. Doodling or drawing may help this process. It is important to objectify your thoughts, so write them down or speak them into a tape recorder (whichever is the least distracting). You may wish to do this as your ideas occur, or stop yourself every twenty minutes or so and record them then. It doesn't matter if they seem far fetched – they can be removed later, as you work through the safeguards listed on pages 53–54.

Having dredged up past dreams, pray about them, asking God to show you why you dismissed them. Often it is because of fear – of our pride, our weaknesses. Do any past dreams reverberate now?

3. Has God given you a hope – for yourself; your family and friends; your church, community or nation? If so, write them down. Then invite the Holy Spirit to fill you with excitement about them and commence the journey of prayer that will lead to their fulfilment. It may help to note any encouragement or signs of progress along the way.

Together

1. Look again at some of the general promises from God (page 51). Discuss together how these impinge on real situations you know, for example, 2 Corinthians 5:1–5 and someone dying of cancer; Romans 8:21 and ecological issues. Then spend time praying for some of these issues and your hopes for them. (Remember; praying also involves listening to God.)

2. In a small group of three or four, offer yourselves to God and invite the Holy Spirit to show you the hope to which God is calling you individually or as a group. After a couple of minutes of quiet and staying open to God's Spirit, ask each person to write down any hopes and dreams they may have for themselves, the church, their family and friends, and their community. After an agreed time (ten minutes or so), take turns to share these thoughts. Respond lovingly to one another, then pray for one another.

Work out a way of going on in prayer together and in discovering God's hopes for each of you. For example, someone's dream for their family might be that the teenage son becomes more responsive towards others in the family. The group might be led to pray for each member of the family, asking for patience and love towards the young person. Another might 'see' what is troubling the teenager, and that could be prayed for. Perhaps someone else has a book on the issue, which they could offer to the family or to other members of the group, to help them pray. One or two in the group may wish to meet regularly with one or more family members to offer support and prayer.

4 PRAYER IN POWER

¹⁹ ...how very great is his power at work in us who believe. This power working in us is the same as the mighty strength ²⁰ which he used when he raised Christ from death and seated him at his right side in the heavenly world. ²¹ Christ rules there above all heavenly rulers, authorities, powers, and lords; he has a title superior to all titles of authority in this world and in the next. ²² God put all things under Christ's feet and gave him to the church as supreme Lord over all things. ²³ The church is Christ's body, the completion of him who himself completes all things everywhere. *(Ephesians 1:19–23)*

Prayer is powerful. It has been described as 'touching the throne of God'. Prayer's power does not reside in us because of who we are or how good we are. Nor is it because we follow the 'right' process or say the 'right' words. The power in prayer resides in God. He is its source, and through prayer his power is released into the situations for which we pray.

We do it all the time without thinking – we switch on the lights, the television, the microwave. But trace the power back to its source – from the switch through the wiring, via the fuse box, out of the home to the local supply system, the substation for the district, across gigantic pylons straddling the horizon, to the power station where millions of kilowatts of power are being generated, enough to light up whole cities and provide the energy for countless factories. When we touch the switch, we are linking in to this enormous reservoir of power – a reservoir about which we normally need to know little.

Paul wanted the Ephesians to know God's power at work in and through them (1:19). Once they could see it and gain some measure of its enormity, they would inevitably begin to sense the importance of prayer. Through prayer, we are given access to God's power. If we trace it back to its source, if we link up all the cable, follow it back through the substation, we will find the mighty strength which God used when he raised Christ from death. This is the power available to us through prayer.

God's power has been demonstrated many times in scripture:

- He can harness the processes of nature and apparently reverse them, for example, delivering Israel from Pharaoh's army as they escaped on the dry sea-bed of the Red Sea (Exod 14).

- He can give life to the dead. This became a powerful metaphor for his ability to revitalise a nation. Ezekiel expresses this in the well-known vision of the Valley of Dry Bones (Ezek 37:4–14).

- He can overcome evil in all its forms – hatred, jealousy, betrayal – even when that evil is institutionalised and energised by satanic forces. He can bring to nothing all global powers, rulers and authorities (Rom 8:38–39).

- He alone has the power to inaugurate the kingdom of God, which he did when he raised Christ to life (Rom 1:2–4).

We need to grasp the greatness of God's power in raising Jesus from the dead. We cannot really comprehend the complexity of the resurrection if we don't. The New Testament makes it plain that Jesus was not only restored to his former human state: there was something transformed and patently glorious about him (Eph 1:22). Furthermore, in restoring Jesus to his rightful supremacy, God dethroned Satan. Such is the power inherent in the resurrection, and, according to Paul, this power can be released in us.

Helen Roseveare, a relatively young missionary doctor, was caught up in the Simba rebellion in the Congo of the mid 1960s.[9] To protect a Greek mother and her newborn baby, Helen stepped out of the security of her house. In response to the thundering knock on the door and the loud demand that she 'open up in the name of the Army of Liberation', she went out pulling the door shut behind her. The angry, anxious, rifle-waving soldiers demanded money. Helen, hardly understanding the language, tried to reason with them. However, the soldiers soon realised that they were not getting what they wanted. Tempers flared quickly and dangerously.

The leader ordered one of his men to strike Helen down. He raised his spear. Something in her froze. Would she live or die? Could she survive the next ten seconds? Was this the end? 'Please, God, if I'm to die, may it be by the first blow!' an agonised gasp heavenward escaped her numb brain, feeling certain that she could not face mutilation. But someone somewhere was praying for her.

After an unbelievably long ten seconds of paralysed time, Helen slowly turned her head. The man stood there, his arm upraised, spear poised to strike, eyes filled with anger, yet unable to move. He was fixed, immobile, arms and legs held as in a vice by a Power that he could neither resist nor overcome.

'Strike her down!' roared the leader to another man. He raised his gun to crash the butt end down on Helen's skull. Again she braced herself for the blow. Everything seemed to be arrested in one long, tortured pause... Again, nothing happened. The second soldier stood as the first, held in the iron grip of an Unseen Force, totally incapable of deliberate movement at the instigation of his own will. Hatred, anger, fear moved across his face.

Helen was suddenly conscious of an overwhelming sense of peace and security and power. Prayer round the world on her behalf had released a mighty outpouring of omnipotence. She was saved. What power could stay the thrust of spear and rifle butt? As Helen reflected on this and many similar experiences, she commented:

> The prayer that was offered on our behalf during the five months of rebel activity in 1964 can never be measured, nor its effectiveness estimated. We only know that God heard and answered. Each one of us, nationals and foreigners, can tell of amazing situations where we were just so conscious of the power of prayer.

Helen's story shows us the power of God at work in and through praying people, and serves to remind us of the variety of ways in which God works. We cannot assume he will act in the way we imagine or the way he has done before. Helen knew people who died 'despite hours of believing prayer ... We did not ask "Why?" but accepted that our God is sovereign.'

To live with God's sovereignty, we need to understand that he operates according to a different set of values from our own. The outcomes may often be perplexing, even to Christians. God's power is always his; it never, ever, becomes ours to use as we want, to claim as our achievement or to satisfy our ambitions. We can only be humble before him.

It is so easy to fall under the illusion that somehow it is *our* energy, *our* obedience, *our* strength, *our* prayers which are affecting things. But we are powerless. We have nothing. God gives all. We are always in the position of the crucified, dead and buried Jesus – utterly dependent on God. Indeed, anytime we begin to think that the power is ours to command or to control, it is likely to cease to operate. Yet God has given us authority to exercise his power according to his will. We have the privilege of pressing the switch.

The Bible is strewn with evidence that God's power is at work in those who believe. The story of Daniel in the lion's den is a familiar one (Dan 6). Darius, the Persian king, is tricked by his officials and governors into issuing a decree that would trap Daniel, an exiled Hebrew foreigner at court, known for his commitment to God and for his faithfulness in prayer. The officials are jealous of Daniel's superior abilities and wish to remove him from the scene altogether. Their plan is to persuade Darius to issue a decree forbidding prayer to any god or man other than himself. Anyone found violating this would be thrown to the lions. Daniel refuses to comply and so is accused by his jealous colleagues. Darius respects and values Daniel, and is deeply distressed, but even he cannot overturn his own law (v 14)! Daniel is thrown to the lions, however much the king does not want to lose his best senior minister. But in the morning the king's anxiety is relieved – Daniel survives:

> [21] 'May Your Majesty live for ever! [22] God sent his angel to shut the mouths of the lions so that they would not hurt me. He did this because he knew that I was innocent and because I have not wronged you, Your Majesty.' *(Daniel 6:21–22)*

Did Daniel pray on this occasion? It would be strange for a man of prayer, like he was, not to do so; but perhaps this isn't the point of the story. Certainly it demonstrates God's amazing power – the lions devour Daniel's accusers when they in turn are thrown into the pit, confirming that it was no accident he survived the night. It also illustrates that God responds to prayer. But who prayed?

> So the king gave orders for Daniel to be arrested and he was thrown into the pit filled with lions. He said to

> Daniel, 'May your God, whom you serve so loyally,
> rescue you.' *(v 16)*

It is the king who breaks his own decree – ironically – and
God answers his prayer!

The story of Nehemiah and the building of the city
walls of Jerusalem gives us a different perspective on
God's power, showing it at work over many months, spanning hundreds of miles, and overcoming all kinds of polit-
ical, social and psychological barriers. As a result,
Nehemiah brings about an extraordinary achievement of
great significance for the people of Israel. But it all begins
with a prolonged time of prayer and fasting (Neh 1).
Nehemiah's prayer is passionate and committed:

> 'Look at me, Lord, and hear my prayer, as I pray day
> and night for your servants, the people of Israel. I
> confess that we, the people of Israel, have sinned. My
> ancestors and I have sinned.' *(v 6)*

We can also see God's power at work in the New
Testament. The healing miracles of Jesus and the disciples reflect closely the power of the resurrection. The
story of Peter's release from prison (Acts 12:6–19) offers
yet another example of God restoring those who are as
good as dead. This story is remarkable not only for its
detail, which reads like 'A Great Escape', but also because
here we see God answering prayer almost in spite of the
'felt' faith of those who prayed! When Peter arrives at the
house where the disciples are praying for his release, he
finds it harder to get in than he did to get out of Herod's
dungeon!

Peter's release underscores this important issue of
God's sovereignty. Immediately preceding this event,
James is arrested and put to death (vs 2–5). Why is it that
James is allowed to be killed while Peter is brought to
safety by miraculous deliverance? The only explanation
left to us is God's sovereignty. (Unless we assume that the
church did not bother to pray for James!)

Our confidence in God's power is firmly grounded in the knowledge that Jesus has given that power to his church, supremely through the gift of the Holy Spirit (Luke 9:1–6; 10:1–12,17–20; 24:45–49; John 20:21–23; Eph 1:23). Standing at the hub of a great electricity station throbbing with power can be both exciting and awe-inspiring. Standing in the presence of God's awesome power is similarly empowering and humbling (Dan 10:16). Both experiences are legitimate. What is not legitimate is that we, the church, fail to acknowledge and release God's power. Our world urgently needs resurrection experiences. We urgently need to pray in power. Here are some ways in which we can do this.

Prayer ideas
Alone

1. Read Ephesians 2:4–6. These verses talk about another resurrection experience, that of coming to new life in Christ. Spend some time thinking about parallel experiences (metaphors), such as rebirth (John 3:3), the germination of a seed (1 Cor 15:35–38), darkness changing to light (Eph 5:8), or even the raising of Lazarus (John 11:38–44). Which experience best fits your own coming to faith? Thank God for his grace towards you. You may find it helpful to write a prayer or letter to God, sketch a picture, write some music, design and sew a piece of cross-stitch, write out an appropriate verse of scripture (using calligraphy), or find some other way to express the significance of your experience. Then offer it to God as a prayer of thanksgiving.

2. Read Ephesians 1:19–20. Look at some artistic depictions of the crucified Jesus (your local library will probably be able to help), or visit churches to see how they depict the brutality and finality of his death. (Where possible, purchase postcards showing these depictions.) As you look at these visual representations, remind yourself of what Paul is saying in the verses you have just read. Thank God that his power brought Jesus gloriously to life. Ask him to help you absorb the truth that this same power is at work in you. Spend time reflecting on what this might mean in your life.

3. Listen to one of the musical representations of the passion and death of Jesus. As you do so, read one or more of the Gospel accounts of the resurrection. In a column down one side of a sheet of paper, list the situations and issues that, to you, seem impossible to change. Opposite your list, in large letters, write the words, 'The power at work in us is the same power of God that raised Christ from death'. Decide on a suitable place to keep your list, where it will encourage you to pray as you live through your difficulties. Ask God to show you how the power of his resurrection love is at work in you.

Together

1. As a group, read Ephesians 2:4–6 to one another in a variety of translations. Another resurrection experience is mentioned here. Give thanks to God for it! It may stimulate thanksgiving and adoration if each of you shares your experiences of this 'spiritual resurrection'.

You could also share with each other the names of people you would like to see coming to faith in Jesus. Pray for their 'resurrection'. It may be useful to keep a list so as to pray for them each time you meet. Keep a note of any progress you discern.

2. 'You have been raised to life ... in heaven, where Christ sits on his throne at the right-hand side of God' (Col 3:1–3). Have any of the group ever been up a high tower, flown in a balloon or travelled by aeroplane? How different did everything seem from such a position? Do such experiences help you understand what Paul meant, or is there more to it? Then, in small groups, share one problem each (either a personal issue or a more general, global one) and ask God to help you see that problem from a heavenly perspective.

Ask God to give you faith that fits his perspective, then seek to pray out of this faith. Don't be disappointed if you don't immediately succeed. Keep going back to seeing the problem from the heavenly perspective and start from there. Let this guide your prayers.

3. Jesus gave us authority and power to command mountains to move (Matt 17:20; Mark 11:12–14, 20–25). John the Baptist, echoing the prophet Isaiah, promised that every hill and mountain which hindered the coming of God's salvation would be removed (Mark 1:2–4; Isaiah 40:3–5). Look together at these scriptures. Try to hear them as the disciples first heard them.

Identify some 'mountains' that hinder God's kingdom coming, perhaps in the life of someone who doesn't believe, perhaps in your church or even your local community. Agree together which issue you will tackle or, if there are several, in which order you want to address them all. Then, together and out loud, command your 'mountains' to move.

If you are new to this kind of praying, it is helpful to discuss your feelings afterwards. Did you feel silly, or did you experience a renewed sense of faith? Try to help each other understand why. Saying commanding prayers often seems to help people focus their prayers. Is this your experience?

4. God's power is at work in us through the Holy Spirit. If we invite God to fill us with the Spirit, we will know his power and use it in prayer. There are many approaches to this. One of these is, first, to invite the Holy Spirit to come to you as a group; then, in turn or as the Holy Spirit directs, pray for each other as individuals. Pray for an increase of faith, boldness, 'felt' power or divine direction. Observe what the Spirit is doing as you pray. When those praying sense that the Spirit has done his work in someone, encourage that person to pray for his or her own individual needs.

5. 'Speak to one another with the words of psalms, hymns, and sacred songs; sing hymns and psalms to the Lord with praise in your hearts' (Eph 5:19). This verse reminds us that there is power in praise (2 Chron 5:11–14; Acts 4:31). There are many ways in which praise can help us experience God's power at work in and through us as we pray. Here are some starter ideas. Why not try one or more of them as you meet over the next few weeks?

- Use spoken and sung praise as prayers.

- Use recordings of praise songs or hymns as a preparation for or background to a time of prayer.

- Memorise verses of psalms or other praise scriptures (or you can read them aloud). Often a verse that one person has chosen will lead others to join in.

Section 2
EPHESIANS 3:14–21

1 FROM THEORY TO PRACTICE

14 For this reason I fall on my knees before the
Father, 15 from whom every family in heaven and on
earth receives its true name. 16 I ask God from the
wealth of his glory to give you power through his
Spirit to be strong in your inner selves, 17 and I pray
that Christ will make his home in your hearts through
faith. I pray that you may have your roots and
foundation in love, 18 so that you, together with all
God's people, may have the power to understand how
broad and long, how high and deep, is Christ's love.
19 Yes, may you come to know his love – although it
can never be fully known – and so be completely
filled with the very nature of God.
     20 To him who by means of his power working in
us is able to do so much more than we can ever ask
for, or even think of: 21 to God be the glory in the
church and in Christ Jesus for all time, for ever and
ever! Amen. *(Ephesians 3:14–21)*

Paul continues to explore the themes of knowing God and
experiencing his power. Once more he paints a large canvas,
spanning heaven and earth, envisaging us ordinary mortals
filled to overflowing with the nature of God! Here again we
see his vision of glory, power, faith, love and the Spirit,
intertwined and shimmering with vibrant colour. A vision to

take our breath away and leave us gasping at its majesty.

It would be a pity to miss the scale and grandeur of Paul's prayer. Why not read the passage again? But this time imagine what it would be like to hear these words if you were a first-century slave, spending your days (and, if required, nights too) at the master's beck and call. In his eyes you are worthless; he bemoans even having to waste money on feeding you.

Picture yourself as a young person today scavenging the rubbish tips in the Philippines, scrapping through other people's rubbish to earn a pittance, eating other people's mouldy food if you are lucky enough to find it. Or as a street child in Guatemala, rejected by your parents and you don't know why, fighting to survive, knowing you are likely to be shot or used for prostitution.

Or come closer to home – you are someone living in a complex western society, the pawn of a market economy, with every advertisement or piece of government legislation aimed at manipulating you for their own ends. As an individual, you only matter to a few (a hundred at the most) people. If you were to die now, what difference would it make?

It is only when we hear Paul's words from such an attitude that we can begin to grasp its true resonance. And these words were written by a man in prison, powerless and doomed. But he is not without God. Awareness of the powerful, loving purposes of God pervades his life.

These verses are almost impossible to analyse. The two main themes, of power and love, flow in and out of one another in a way which is, for me, rather like riding a carousel at the fair ground – nothing stays still long enough to be sure what I am seeing. The whole passage is shot through with strong emotion, even passion. It is possible, however, to distinguish three parts – an introduction (vs 14–15), the prayer itself (vs 16–19) and, finally, the doxology (vs 20– 21).

The introduction looks backward ('For this reason') and

upward (to 'the Father'). We look backward to the whole plan of God the Father, whose purpose is to bring us all into his family (1:5). We look upward to God the Father 'from whom every family in heaven and on earth receives its true name' (4:15).[10] Again we find, to our surprise, that both roads lead to the same point – our relationship with God. We are his children.

The doxology is staggering in its vision. It is like standing on a mountain-top, trying to take in at a glance the entire panorama lying before us – lakes, majestic trees, colourful birds, exotic flowers, towering mountains, meandering rivers. It draws together so much of what Paul has already unpacked – God's power, the richness of his plans and purposes, his achievements in us, his glory, the church, Christ and eternity. God's 'power working in us is able to do so much more than we can ever ask for, or even think of' (3:20). Perhaps it is all too much to grasp at once. This doxology functions like an impressionist painting. Although we may try to make sense of it, part of its power – indeed, part of its meaning – is bound up in the fact that we cannot see everything with clarity. Absorbing the overall vision is more important than scouring for details. What could be more appropriate for a God who cannot be fully known!

Let us now explore the core prayer more closely. Paul is almost halfway through his letter and about to move from stating the principles of faith to seeing how that faith is worked out in daily life. (Ephesians 4 marks a clear transition from belief to behaviour.) But before he goes on to exhort the Ephesians to live the faith, he first prays for them. He does this because he knows that they will need to draw on all the resources available to them if they are to live lives that fully reflect the qualities God's people should have. He also knows that the demands of living for Christ will be costly. Only through the Spirit will they be empowered to live out their faith (3:16–19). Strength comes through the Spirit; Christ's presence comes through faith; love comes through understanding. Once again we glimpse the shimmering perspective of Paul's life in God. Once again we see how his prayer flows out of his passionate engagement with God's plan (3:11-12).

Ephesus was a pagan city, exciting, dangerous and immoral. But throughout Paul's letter to the Ephesian church is a wonderful sense of Christ's victory over the pagan world. Paul takes seriously his calling to bring the gospel to the Gentiles, which he regards as a divinely given privilege (3:1,6-7). Now that his evangelism in Ephesus has been halted by his imprisonment, he can still work out this privilege by praying for the Christians there. He may be in prison, but he can still pray with absolute commitment and thus fulfil his God-given task. Paul knows that God has redeemed the Gentile Ephesians in Christ and given them his Spirit as their guarantee. So now he prays that they will fully realise God's plan in their lives. Knowing God and knowing them gives him reason to pray and helps him know how to pray.

The opening words of the introduction, 'For this reason', reiterate what has become a recurring motif in this epistle: Paul uses the phrase four times, all in the context of prayer (1:15; 3:1,14; 6:18). Is this perhaps to emphasise, amidst the supernatural power and wonder that suffuses his letter, that there is also a logical process to prayer? 'For this reason' implies that when we pray, we need to use our minds (1 Cor 14:15), illuminated by our place in God's kingdom and opened to the Spirit's insight. Then our prayers will have focus and the power that comes from our partnership with God. If we want to follow Paul and pray 'for this reason', there are four aspects we may need to keep in mind.

First, we require *information*. It helps to have as clear a picture as possible of any situation for which we pray. What is going on? How are the people involved? Are they quarrelling, confused, elated, discouraged? Are they starving, busy, ill, successful? Paul was always keen to discover as much as possible about other people's circumstances. It was hearing about the Ephesians' faith that prompted him to pray (1:15). We often find gathering information off-putting, 'boring' even, but once we understand that it is the basic fuel for prayer, we will view it differently.

However, we need more than information – we need *insight*. Having discovered all we can about a situation, we need to ask, 'Why is it like this?' Sometimes this question will receive answers at a physical, human level; sometimes we need to move into the spiritual realms in order to understand why things are as they are. Job's friends knew what had happened to Job at one level, but they struggled to respond appropriately because they were, unfortunately, unaware of the spiritual reasons behind Job's suffering.

Once we gain some idea of the what and the why, we need to place it alongside God's revealed purposes and be guided by the Holy Spirit so as to determine how to pray. This third aspect I call *inspiration*. It is not just about understanding a particular situation from God's perspective; it is also about inviting him to reveal his will for that situation and agreeing with him that this is what we want, too. This may sound logical, but it often does not appear that way, not least because it will often be directly opposed to Satan's will and will therefore appear 'unreasonable' (Matt 5:43–45). Furthermore, because we will be in conflict with Satan, our wills may soon grow weary unless we seek the continuing inspiration of God to strengthen us.

The final aspect of reasonable prayer is *involvement*. When we are clear as to what God's will on earth is for a specific situation, we still need to know what our part in that may be. We may, for instance, recognise that it is God's will to meet the needs of homeless people. We may appreciate that one way to do this is to utilise a bus as a mobile feeding and medical centre. When we are sure this is what God wants, we still have to decide what our role is. To buy the food, cook it or distribute it? Or should we child-mind so that someone else can drive the bus? Normally, when we discover our particular involvement, we will be able to make our contribution effectively and consistently. The same is true of prayer. Often our proper involvement will be linked to our relationship with people, our role in the situation and our gifting.

Paul sees himself, not as the prisoner of Caesar nor of Rome, but as 'the prisoner of Christ Jesus' (Eph 3:1). He is detained at his divine majesty's pleasure. Jesus, not Caesar, is Lord, even in those restricting, exacting circumstances. We may feel that our own circumstances are a prison-like trap which hinder or even prevent us from getting on with God's work. But we need to be clear both about God's general call on our lives, and what he has appointed us to do. Collectively, we are all called to make disciples of 'all peoples' and to let our light shine so that people glorify God (Matt 5:16; 28:19). Individually, many of us have a personal sense of what God is asking us to do and be. God's purpose for us at each moment lies somewhere at the intersection of these two factors. The general call (to make disciples) can serve as a focus for our individual call and provide us with a compelling motivation to pray.

For example, if you are a parent, the outworking of God's general call on your life will be the spiritual nurture of your children. You are a 'prisoner of Christ Jesus' for their sake. For this reason, you may want to pray specifically for them and their individual circumstances. So, if they are very young, you might want to pray that they will grow into a sense of wonder as they become more and more aware of the world, or that they will experience God's love through your loving service. If they are facing problems, you might want to pray that they will learn through the experience and grow nearer to God, that they will be protected from harm spiritually or physically, and that your love will mirror God's patience. The situation may sometimes feel like imprisonment to you, but when you perceive it as Paul does, it will help to motivate you to deeper levels of prayer and clarify the direction in which to pray. Besides which, as you pray, a real sense of partnership with God may develop.

This attitude should pervade our concerns for all those we are in relationship with – other Christians, an unbelieving partner, our colleagues at work, our city or country. Whenever we find ourselves knowing God's call on our lives but apparently unable to fulfil that calling, we are God's prisoners. We are not the prisoners of the problem – of a bad marriage, elderly parents, unemployment. We are 'prisoners of Christ Jesus'. He is in the situation with us. He is Lord of it. He has not revoked his claim on our lives. We can work through anything with him in prayer. If we proceed first by thinking things through and then experiment by praying over those issues, God will show us the next step. In this way any kind of prayer for others can develop into a significant adventure with God.

If we believe that God is worth knowing and, more amazingly, that he wants to know us, then prayer makes sense. Most Christians have to cope sooner or later with comments like, 'If he is God, doesn't he already know what you want?' 'If he is good, won't he give you what you need anyway, without you having to ask?' 'If it's not for your good, it would be better not to ask in the first place!' I suspect we have sometimes asked ourselves, 'Just what am I doing talking to myself? Am I going mad?' It may sometimes feel as though we are muttering absentmindedly or talking our heads off for no apparent reason. But these arguments miss the point entirely. Prayer is more about relating than getting or not getting. In prayer, we are talking to God, sharing our deepest concerns with him. Paradoxically, whatever happens after our prayers, we do get the most important thing in life – quality time with God:

> The key Christian insight about intimacy is that it is a
> characteristic of our relationship with God. In the
> presence of God we are laid bare before him ... Those

who have faith in God and spend time in the presence
of God know that this relationship of faith is the way
in which all other relationships start to fall into place.
(Roy McCloughry) [11]

Prayer puts us in the position of having to admit to ourselves that God is absolutely necessary and we cannot do
much without him. Human beings have a tendency to
think that we are the movers and shakers of the universe.
Prayer enables us to live with the truth that it is God and
only God who counts. Prayer is a powerful way of living in
this truth, which is vital for a healthy, growing faith. It is
the way we begin to put our theoretical faith into practice.

Prayer ideas
Alone
1. Do you think prayer is a reasonable pursuit for
Christians? If so, why? If not, why not? For most of us, our
feelings vary, so try to work out why sometimes you feel
it's OK and why sometimes you feel awkward about it.
(Has anyone, especially someone you respected or loved,
mocked you for praying?) Make a list of all the factors that
make prayer reasonable for you. Thank God for who he is
and for his truth. Then list all the issues you think someone who considers prayer irrational might raise. Invite
God to show you how you could deal with these objec-
tions (Eph 1:16–19).

2. What circumstances come nearest in your experience
to imprisonment? Are they temporary or permanent? Do
you believe that you should pray for release from your
'imprisonment' (Acts 12), or do you need to accept that
you are a 'prisoner of Christ Jesus'? If the latter, how can
your 'imprisonment' lead to effective prayer?

3. Read Genesis 13:12–13; 18:16–33; 19:23–29. Work out
what information, insight, inspiration and involvement
Abraham had which led him to pray as he did.

4. Using the simple chart on page 81, work through some issues you have prayed for and see to what extent, in practice, you have already prayed using the ways described on pages 74–76. Apply them to some concerns you have at the moment and see if it helps you to pray with greater depth. Remember, it is often in the process of praying that we begin to see more clearly how to pray. It may also be that you discover something fairly simple, such as, 'It might help to gather more information'.

Together

1. Share insights from books or sermons that have helped you to cope with the sense that prayer might be childish or irrational. Pray for each other, that you may have a sense that prayer is a mature (and maturing) partnership with God. Thank God for the life of Jesus and the part that prayer played in it.

2. Do you find information a help or a hindrance in prayer? How is it most helpful to you to receive information? Talk through these perspectives together, then pray for a situation where you have lots of information and for a situation where your knowledge is very restricted. Share your responses to these prayer experiences. You could also keep a check on how your prayers are answered. Do you feel that our lack of information hinders God?

3. If you are with a group of people you trust, you may find it helpful to talk through your responses in the chart in No. 4 'Alone' above. You will probably discover that some people find factual information helpful/necessary/motivational, while others enjoy the inspirational aspects of prayer. Still others are better at working out the more practical aspects – what involvement they should have in a situation and how this gives clarity to their prayers. So why not work as a team on some shared prayer issues?

4. Individually, think of three situations in your life that feel like 'imprisonment'. (They can be temporary, like the car being out of action, or much more permanent, like serious arthritis that restricts mobility. They can also be emotional things, like depression or personality factors.) Share one item each with the group, then pray for each other that somehow Jesus will show you how he can use the situation to further his purposes.

Invite individuals to each share one of the remaining two situations that seem like 'imprisonment'. Then help each other to see how these appear to hinder what you sense God is calling you to be and do. Finally, discover together how, through prayer, you can circumvent the problem (for example, Paul prayed for the Christians in Ephesus even though he could not preach the gospel there).

Take a large piece of paper (flip-chart size) and, in the middle, write the word 'prisoners'. From this centre, draw spokes and join the spokes with an outer circle. Around the outer circle write, 'Jesus is Lord'. Invite individual group members to write on one of the spokes their third 'imprisonment' situation. Ask people to pray silently and lovingly for one another's concerns, perhaps by pointing to the appropriate spoke. Encourage them to listen to God for one another. (For example, how does God see this situation? What might be his solution? Should we pray for release from 'imprisonment'). Finally, invite the group to share any reflections they may have. Obviously, it is important to avoid creating feelings of condemnation, so encourage people to share things positively and gently.

	Answered prayers	**Issues I am praying for**
Information		
Insight		
Inspiration		
Involvement		

2 PASSION IN PRAYER

For this reason I fall on my knees before the Father...
(Ephesians 3:14)

In the last chapter we saw some of the more practical aspects of Paul's approach to prayer. His demonstrative commitment is not surprising in one who believed in God so strongly and who was as involved in God's concerns as Paul was. However, the balance to loving God with all our mind is to love him with our heart and strength. This is reflected in Paul's comment in verse 14. Unusually, he refers to his posture in prayer. Does he 'fall on his knees' because of the earnestness of his praying or because of who he knows God to be? Is it because he is overwhelmed by God's glory, grace and greatness? It is not difficult to think that the latter might be a major cause of his abandoned approach to prayer. But there is no sense that this is some kind of unwilling submission. Kneeling seems to be the physical sign of his glad but ultimate surrender, born of awe and love, nurtured in devotion and intimacy, the fullest physical expression of spiritual adoration and passion. Such passion overflows to include those whom God loves.

Sometimes, probably more often than we allow, we should let our prayers be driven by love for others, a sense of desperate need and a faith which somehow knows that 'God can do it when no one else can'. Maybe you are cautious about expressing your emotions in your prayer-life, perhaps worried that you will look foolish or that others will think you are overreacting. Indeed, emotional outbursts can be a cheap alternative to practical commitment, or a cover-up (even if a subconscious one) for suppressed guilt; so a degree of self-control may well be a good thing. But, then again, it may not be. We have to take risks sometimes.

A child is swept along in a flood-swollen river, with little hope of survival. Driven by love, her father abandons all caution and jumps in to rescue her. Often we would do better in God's sight to become actively involved in the rescue operation, than to work out beforehand a precise analysis as to why we think rescue might be a good thing! How free are we from our selfish needs and ambitions to feel this passionately about other people's needs and situations? Are we so committed to God's cause that it matters desperately when situations seem to reflect adversely on his honour? What do we do when the life of our church, our society, our world casts shadows on the glory of God?

Jairus was 'an official in the local synagogue'. His only daughter was dying and he was desperate enough to throw himself at Jesus' feet (Luke 8:40–56). Every word of the account in the Gospel underlines the pressure he was under. Surrounded by crowds of people, all of whom probably knew him, not for Jairus the comfort and convenience of revealing his vulnerability in private (contrast the story of Nicodemus in John 3:1–2). Most of us find it easier to demonstrate our emotions away from public view, preferably among strangers, where if we make a fool of ourselves, we at least won't have to live with the consequences, and the faces we see every day won't remind us of our foolish extravagance. Nevertheless, Jairus 'threw himself down at Jesus' feet and begged him to go to his home'. There is nothing measured here, no restraint or calculated diplomacy. Rather, Jairus was a man driven by passionate concern for his daughter. He completely forgot who he was in his desperation and his total conviction that only Jesus could save the situation. With the benefit of hindsight, it may not seem so shocking to us; but for the onlookers, who may not have known Jairus' circumstances, it may have seemed a little over the top!

I suspect that as Jairus flung himself before Jesus, he neither saw nor heard anyone else. He knelt in desperation, but people 'fall on their knees' for all kinds of reasons. In the book of Revelation, the twenty-four elders knelt in adoration and awe (Rev 4:9–11), prompted by the praise of the four living creatures. When John saw the glorified Christ, he too fell down, but this time out of fear (Rev 1:17; see also Luke 8:47). 'Felt weakness' is another emotion that brings people to their knees. At the end of a marathon, the runners collapse in a heap as they cross the finishing line. Sometimes when we come to God in prayer, we may feel that we have carried the burden as long as we can and now have to place it in God's hands.

> [28] 'Come to me, all of you who are tired from carrying heavy loads, and I will give you rest. [29] Take my yoke and put it on you, and learn from me, because I am gentle and humble in spirit; and you will find rest. [30] For the yoke I will give you is easy, and the load I will put on you is light.' *(Matthew 11:28–30)*

In this picture, Jesus is depicting himself as the mature ox and us as the calf in training. When we take his yoke and put it on, although we may feel we are taking on extra weight we are actually taking on his strength. All his power and stamina will be transferred to the plough; all his might will help us pull the load along. This is what happens when we surrender in prayer to God.

Sometimes we western, cerebral Christians find it difficult to comprehend how much our bodies reflect our emotions, and not just our emotions but our wills, too. In worship and in prayer we need to be free to say what we mean with our bodies as well as with our words. Whether it be in silence or tongues, in raising our hands or opening them before God, in kneeling or dancing, by weeping or laughing, fasting or feasting, with others or by ourselves, our bodies as much as our spirits have a message to give to God. So we can pray with our bodies – indeed, sometimes this is the only adequate language.

We do sometimes put our bodies through some strange contortions when we pray! Most of us will have heard of the term 'shampoo praying' – heads down in our hands, rubbing our hair. Nevertheless, our failure to involve our bodies can indicate barriers, conscious or not, in our openness to God and our commitment to the gospel. Becoming aware of where and how our bodies are resistant can teach us a lot about our relationship with God. Conversely, saying to God we are willing and expressing this level of obedience through our bodies can become a significant breakthrough for our spirits.

We ignore our bodies in worship at our peril. Body language is important in the spiritual realm as well as the interpersonal one. Certainly we can train our bodies to lie to God without realising it. We can also sing endlessly about 'kneeling' and 'lifting our hands' without really doing it. 'What is the harm?' we ask ourselves. When Paul tells us that he 'falls to his knees' in prayer for the Ephesians, he presents a challenge to those following the man whose obedience to God found its expression in a physical, bodily act – death on a cross.

When we 'fall on our knees', we are essentially doing two things. First, we are abandoning our selves, our dignity, our self-centredness and our self-protection to God. Second, we are affirming God's sufficiency. He is able to handle our circumstances and we can totally release them to him. These actions place us in a powerful place for prayer.

Some things you can only see from your knees. Coventry Cathedral is well-known for its striking modern architecture. One of its most notable features is the huge tapestry of the ascended Christ which dominates the nave, filling the space from floor to ceiling behind the altar. However, on occasions, the great baptismal window can be just as powerful. It was once my privilege to take the early morning communion service in the Chapel of Unity, a small circular side chapel situated opposite the baptismal window, the entrance to which is up some steps and through a small doorway leading off the main body of the church. One day, after receiving the bread and wine, I knelt down. As I did so, the early morning sun shone through the window, causing it to glow incandescently. If I had not knelt down, I might have missed the whole thing and never have seen it as it was meant to be seen. I have carried with me a sense of 'the heavens opening' ever since.

Do we really need to kneel to pray, or is this only a matter of personal preference? To be honest, I have no way of being sure whether or not Paul meant that he was physically on his knees. However, kneeling is a powerful expression of our surrender to God.[12] Of course, there is the danger that we turn the symbolic act into empty routine. Graham Kendrick tells an amusing story of a young boy's first visit to the local parish church:[13]

> On entering the church, the boy was instantly curious, fascinated by this strange new world. The hushed voices, the high arches, the slightly musty smell and the rows of empty wooden pews. Or were they empty? No, here and there a hat, the back of a head, a pair of hunched shoulders, would bob up or down, appear or disappear.
>
> His mother led him in whispers to one of these dark tunnel like rows, where she immediately knelt and bowed her head; he copied instinctively. The silence only lasted for a few more seconds, as the question that had been growing more and more

urgent in his lively young mind suddenly burst out,
ringing loud and clear through the ancient arches:
'Mummy, who are we all hiding from?'

There are other ways of expressing how we feel in prayer.
While our culture is inclined to reject formalities such as
bowing, saluting or even shaking hands, people do need
and welcome ways of communicating physically. (Think,
for instance, of the way in which 'hugs' have often
replaced handshakes!) Sometimes 'to stand up' may be a
better acknowledgment of our awe in God's presence.
What about 'lifting our voices in praise'? Or expressing
our praise, or our submission, with our hands? Most of us
will probably know of times when our hearts have not
been in the least bit inclined to praise God – but, as we
expressed praise through our voices as an act of will, our
hearts were set free. If we don't express our praise with
our voices when we can, something atrophies within us.

There is room – indeed, a need – for us to show our passion in our praying. If prayer is limited by what is 'reasonable', it is in danger of becoming cold and uncommit-
ted as we withhold the full surrender of our wills and
emotions to the purposes of God. However, if prayer is all
passion, it may well end up superficial or selfish. In praying, passion and reason belong together. When the power
of each is harmonised with the other, the result is a God-
focused, people-sensitive, rich prayer-life. We cannot
pray with our whole being unless both our reason and our
emotion are available to God.

Prayer ideas
Alone

1. 'Love the Lord your God with all your heart, with all
your soul, and with all your mind' (Matt 22:37). To what
extent do you find that praying engages 'all of your mind
and all of your heart'? Write down five ways in which you
could involve the mind in prayer and five ways in which

you could involve the heart. How many of these ways do you use in prayer? Does this suggest that you need to work more on reason or more on passion in your praying? Is the balance a reflection of your personality and gifting, or does it indicate other factors which need attention?

2. Try singing a song or hymn from the perspectives of different Bible characters – for example, the hymn 'You are the King of Glory' could be sung from the perspective of those welcoming Jesus into Jerusalem, the women kneeling before the cross, or the disciples greeting the Risen Lord for the first time. Use your imagination or various bodily positions to help you get into these differing perspectives. How does it affect the significance of what you are singing? Does it add to, or detract from, the meaning of the words?

3. Try kneeling down. What different positions can you occupy? Do you feel physical discomfort, odd? You may be asking, 'What am I doing this for? Do I look stupid?' Imagine someone coming in to the room right now. What do you think you would feel like?

Have you reached the point of being able to kneel in prayer? What does this contribute to your prayer experience?

Together

1. Discuss whether or not you find it easy to express spiritual reality in physical ways. Are you aware of any barriers? Would it help to try to worship God in dance? Can you use physical movements of the hands or the whole body in worship songs? Have you ever tried fasting? If not, why not?

2. Look through some worship songs together and discuss how many references there are to physical expressions. Do you think that using actions complement the words of the song or not? What hinders us (inhibitions, awareness of other people, the constraints of the building and seating)?

Work out physical ways of expressing any actions described in the song. Does doing them enhance the reality you are singing about (for example, 'raising hands', 'lifting the name', 'clapping' or 'celebrating'). If you feel comfortable doing this, perhaps individual group members could perform these actions in front of the group. Then compare your experiences and responses.

3. Sit or stand in a circle, holding hands. Try to communicate joy, love, tenderness, strength through the ways you hold each other's hands. Then relax and quietly pray first for the person on your right and then for the person on your left. The group leader can then invite open prayer for various individuals in the circle.

After a time of quiet, the leader invites the group to move closer together and to place their arms around one another. Perhaps you could say the grace together (2 Cor 13:13) or some other short, affirming prayer. Finally, join hands but remain close to each other. Raise your hands to form a crown, while someone reads a passage such as 1 Peter 2:9–10 or Revelation 5:11–14.

Perhaps time for reflection and discussion on this experience will be helpful. Does such a physical expression of corporateness help or hinder the reality of togetherness in prayer? Listening to how others have benefited from or struggled with these experiences may give you a greater understanding of why others in your church or group do things differently from you. Use this as a learning experience not only for yourself and what you find useful, but also as a tool for understanding, accepting and assisting each other. In this way you can move towards greater freedom of physical expression in prayer.

3 A HOME FOR CHRIST

I pray that Christ will make his home in your hearts
through faith. *(Ephesians 3:17)*

As a travelling preacher, I am often invited to stay in people's homes. I can tell you they are all very different – in size, situation, decor and tidiness. But I always consider it a privilege to be allowed to stay – there are always things to enjoy, discoveries to make. To share a family's home for a day or two means being allowed into the heart of that family. Of course, it is possible that they are on their best behaviour for a couple of days while I'm around! But every family who gives me hospitality knows they run the risk of my finding out 'what they're really like' – especially if they have small children who can let out the family secrets!

Over the years I have also come to realise, somewhat to my surprise, that people have felt it a privilege to have me in their homes. Undoubtedly, the first Christians would have felt this way toward the great apostle. Paul, on his travels, spent a lot of time staying in other people's homes (Acts 16:15), so when he writes about Christ making 'his home in your hearts', he is drawing on his own experiences of being made to feel welcomed and loved by his many hosts. Probably, during his time in Ephesus, he stayed with that warm and hospitable couple, Priscilla and Aquila, as Apollos had done earlier (18:24 – 19:10). I have little doubt that his appreciation of the privilege was similar to my own. It is wonderful to know you have somewhere to stay and someone to belong to, however short or long your visit. Paul certainly knew the blessing it was to give and receive hospitality, especially over an extended period. Sometimes it was a matter of life and death; at other times, simply a great opportunity to share the riches of being an ambassador for Christ. What stories his hosts must have heard!

It is worth noting that in the Greek, just one word is used for the phrase 'make his home' – *katoikeo*:

> There are two similar Greek verbs, *paroikeo* and *katoikeo*. The former is the weaker. It means to inhabit (a place) as a stranger, to live in fact as a *paroikos*, the very word Paul has used in 2.19 for an alien who is living away from his home. *Katoikeo*, on the other hand, means to settle down somewhere. It refers to a permanent as opposed to a temporary abode, and is used metaphorically both for the fullness of the Godhead abiding in Christ and for Christ's abiding in the believer's heart. ... Paul prays to the Father that Christ by his Spirit will be allowed to settle down in their hearts, and from his throne there both control and strengthen them. *(John Stott)* [14]

Paul is describing something far longer than my brief Sunday stay when he prays for Christ to make his home with us. He is thinking of long-term residency. He wants to prepare Christians to be God's permanent dwelling place, rather than a temporary one like a tent. Nevertheless, we should bear in mind the significance of God's 'sacred tent' in the Old Testament (Exod 25:8; 29:42–46). God's presence made 'the Tent and the altar holy', and his presence ensured that the people knew he was the God who had redeemed them from Egypt. Paul is developing his earlier idea that all Christians become a 'sacred temple dedicated to the Lord' (Eph 2:20–22). God will live in them and they will know him. They will be 'completely filled with the very nature of God' (Eph 3:19), as the newly consecrated Tent and later the Temple were filled with the glory of God (1 Kings 8:10–13).

There are many accounts in the Gospels of Jesus staying in people's homes. As we look at these, one of the first things to note is how varied those homes were. Simon Peter's home was a very ordinary one in the Galilean fishing town of Capernaum – the equivalent today might be a three-bedroom semi in the suburbs (Mark 1:29–31). The home of Mary, Martha and Lazarus was probably very different (Luke 10:38–41; John 11:1). Bethany was a suburb for the affluent who wanted to be near Jerusalem but not to live among its crowded, confined streets. From what we know of Martha, it is all too easy to surmise that the house was neat, pretentious and over-fastidious! Perhaps the equivalent today would be a renovated country mansion or Cotswold cottage. Matthew and Zacchaeus were both tax collectors (Matt 9:9–13; Luke 19:1–10). Both appear to have had fairly large houses, where a great number of people could congregate. Jesus visited Zacchaeus's home without any warning, giving Zacchaeus no time to make special preparations. Matthew's invitation was to a party for all his friends who, it appears, were not the most refined crowd around!

Jesus seems to have felt at home in all kinds of company, in small and large houses, whether the visit was planned or hasty. So we do not need to worry too much about the kind of people we think we are – Christ can still 'make his home' in our hearts, and we can still enjoy his friendship.

The needs that brought Jesus to people's homes were also varied. Usually he went only when asked, as with Jairus; but sometimes he invited himself, as with Zacchaeus, and sometimes he went apparently for his own convenience, as with the home where the last supper was convened. Again, we can be reassured that the formalities didn't matter to him. He will come whether or not we ask him, whether or not we are feeling our best, in times of crisis or on more mundane occasions. Whatever the circumstances, he wants to enter the homes of our hearts.

When Jesus visited people's homes, his being there was usually a notable, often life-changing occasion. If it was a great and memorable event for Jesus to visit someone's home, how much more so is his presence at the centre of our lives through the abiding presence of the Holy Spirit:

> [10] But it was to us that God made known his secret by means of his Spirit. The Spirit searches everything, even the hidden depths of God's own purposes. [11] It is only the spirit within people that knows all about them; in the same way, only God's Spirit knows all about God. [12] We have not received this world's spirit; instead, we have received the Spirit sent by God, so that we may know all that God has given us.
> *(1 Corinthians 2:10–12)*

The presence of Christ in our hearts, through the Holy Spirit, gives us access to the mind of God. Furthermore, whereas now our knowledge of God is only partial, God's knowledge of us is complete (1 Cor 13:12). Through Christ being at home in our hearts, we are being known more deeply, being loved more dearly, being guarded more tenderly than we are probably aware of.[15]

Of course, the word 'heart' is not here referring to the organ that pumps the blood round the body! It is difficult to determine its full meaning, though it conjures up a powerful image. 'The heart' is often used to describe what lies at the centre of the human soul. Thus we say ,'I love you with all my heart', a statement that surely incorporates more than just the emotions but the mind and the will, too. In Ephesians 1:18, the Greek says, 'that *the eyes of your heart* may be enlightened so that you may know...' The *Good News Bible* translates the phrase in italics as 'mind'. In Ephesians 6:5, Paul instructs slaves to be obedient with 'a sincere heart', which amounts to 'with a devoted will'. But in Ephesians 5:19, we are to 'sing hymns and psalms to the Lord with praise in your hearts', which includes emotional intensity.

'The heart' is a term that seems to capture the core reality of a person. If Christ is in our hearts, then his presence will affect all of our life and all that flows from us. People may not know what is hidden at the centre of our being, but his presence there will make a difference to what they sense – everything we are, say, do and touch. This surely shows that Paul's prayer that Christ will make his home in our hearts is not just that we will be aware of Christ's presence but also transformed into his character. It is not just that we achieve personal completion but have a profound effect on those around us. When we manifest Christ's love, we are experiencing him living in us and through us as his love flows out of us towards others. Note how Paul keeps returning to the fact of Christ's love working its way through in the daily living of believers:

> Instead, by speaking the truth in a spirit of love, we must grow up in every way to Christ, who is the head. *(4:15)*

> Instead, be kind and tender-hearted to one another, and forgive one another, as God has forgiven you in Christ. *(4:32)*

> Your life must be controlled by love, just as Christ loved us and gave his life for us... *(5:2)*

> Submit yourselves to one another because of your reverence for Christ. *(5:21)*

> ...with all your heart, do what God wants, as slaves to Christ. *(6:6)*

Now we begin to see what a positive and powerful effect this brief prayer can have on someone's life. If they are depressed, to pray that they will have Christ in their heart is to ask that their self-worth be restored, their anger dissolved and that they be released from the darkness which oppresses them. If someone is finding a situation at work problematic, to pray that they will have Christ in their heart is to desire that they be set free from fear and gain new energy to be positive, to serve, perhaps even to make a stand for integrity. Praying that Christ has a home in someone's heart means asking for Christ to make his salvation real for that person and for their circumstances. It will have life-changing consequences for them and for those around them.

So often prayer is about making clearer what is already present, about bringing what is indistinct into focus. Jesus is already present in the Christian's life, but we still need to ask that his presence will be more fully appreciated. Like the shimmering, shifting images of a reflection in a pond, where the water is broken by the ripples caused by the wind blowing, we only understand partially the power of the presence of the exalted Christ in us. Throughout Ephesians, the themes of Christ's power and his love are entwined. When Christ makes his home in our hearts, the inner person which has been distorted by pressures from within and without is restored by his love and his power.

It is his love that motivates him to set up a home in our hearts; it is his power that empowers us to love. Through his presence in us, the power of perfect love is released. This perfect love transforms sin into goodness, casts out fear and failure, brings delight and wholeness (*shalom*). This perfect love energises, motivates, envisions. It releases compassion and righteousness. It will empower the Ephesians to live the lives that Paul will go on to explore in detail in chapters 4–6 of his letter, where he calls on them to live for Christ at work, in the family and in the wider society.

Prayer ideas

Alone

1. Imagine you have recently married someone and are moving into his or her home. Look around at the decor, the furnishings and equipment. Some things you probably consider great; some things you would say to yourself, 'I can't live with that!' Some things, you decide, will need altering over the course of months or even years. Because you love this person, you don't want to upset them. But still some things must change.

Now imagine that Christ is coming into your life to make his home in your heart. Invite the Holy Spirit to show you what changes Christ wants to make, what aspects of you he really approves and what will need altering over the years. Please know that Christ loves you, loves you enough to give his life for you. He certainly doesn't want to harm or hurt you. He is also the perfect gentleman and will not intrude uninvited. So try not to be anxious as he looks around your life. Take note of what he shows you. If possible, talk and pray these things through with a friend.

You may also wish to go a step further. It is not hard to imagine how alterations to your new partner's home might improve both their surroundings and their enjoyment of life; how much more will the changes that Christ makes improve the quality of our lives. What might his cleansing, rearranging, removing and refurbishing of your life mean for you? (Your greatest benefit will be his presence in fuller measure.)

2. Christ at home in our hearts means love operating in our relationships. Pray through some of your relationships, first drawing on the supplies of Christ's love, as follows.

Read some passages about Christ loving you, such as John 3:14–16; 13:1–9; Romans 5:5–11; 1 Corinthians 13;

2 Corinthians 5:14–15; 1 Peter 1:3–5; 1 John 4:9–12. As you read each one, thank Jesus and accept his love. Ask the Holy Spirit to pour Christ's love into your heart (Rom 5:5). If it helps, imagine this process as a glass being filled from a jug of wine.

Then pray for your marriage partner, your office colleagues, your teacher, your awkward teenage child, the person under you who won't co-operate, and so on. Ask God to show you how to love them with Christ's love.

3. Draw the axes of a graph as below. Write on each axis appropriate expressions of your experiences of Christ's love. Then thank God for them. Words may not be enough – music, art, silence, body positions can all be used.

Height

Breadth

Length

Depth

Together

1. As a church or prayer group, pray for:

- The family of the church in its different departments, for example, the music ministry, children's work, care of the premises, administration, mission and outreach.

- Families in the church, especially those with special needs (but be careful *not* to breach confidentiality in this process).

Pray that Christ will make his home in these situations. What differences do you think his being there will make? Pray that they will become a reality. (It may be appropriate to prayerfully discuss these differences before you pray.)

2. Worship is a key opportunity for the church to affirm, recognise and experience that Christ is making his home in our hearts. Thank God for such experiences and pray for those who have the responsibility of planning and leading worship.

3. Look at No. 3 'Alone' above. Work on the graph from the point of view of the church as a whole. Can your group come up with a visual way (a video 'clipboard', a poster, a photographic compilation) that will help the church to appreciate Christ's love for them and through them? Now add to the graph ways in which you would like the love of Christ to be expressed in each dimension. Commit yourselves to pray for these to happen.

Section 3
EPHESIANS 6:10–22

1 FROM PRAYING TO PLEADING

Our journey in prayer is moving towards its final phase. We have now explored two of the main 'prayer islands' in Ephesians (1:15–23; 3:14–21), and traversed the straits which lead us there (1:1–14). Only one island remains: our final major passage is 6:10–22. As before, we begin by looking at the map and doing a quick circumnavigation before we go on to make a more detailed exploration.

> 10 Finally, build up your strength in union with the Lord and by means of his mighty power. 11 Put on all the armour that God gives you, so that you will stand up against the Devil's evil tricks. 12 For we are not fighting against human beings but against the wicked spiritual forces in the heavenly world, the rulers, authorities, and cosmic powers of this dark age. 13 So take up God's armour now! Then when the evil day comes, you will be able to resist the enemy's attacks; and after fighting to the end, you will still hold your ground.
> 14 So stand ready, with truth as a belt tight round your waist, with righteousness as your breastplate, 15 and as your shoes the readiness to announce the Good News of peace. 16 At all times carry faith as a shield; for with it you will be able to put out all the burning arrows shot by the Evil One. 17 And accept salvation as a helmet, and the word of God as the

sword which the Spirit gives you. [18] Do all this in
prayer, asking for God's help. Pray on every occasion,
as the Spirit leads. For this reason keep alert and
never give up; pray always for all God's people.
[19] And pray also for me, that God will give me a
message when I am ready to speak, so that I may
speak boldly and make known the gospel's secret.
[20] For the sake of this gospel I am an ambassador,
though now I am in prison. Pray that I may be bold in
speaking about the gospel as I should.
  [21] Tychicus, our dear brother and faithful servant
in the Lord's work, will give you all the news about
me, so that you may know how I am getting on.
[22] That is why I am sending him to you – to tell you
how all of us are getting on, and to encourage you.
(Ephesians 6:10–22)

Straight away we can see that this is a large island. Part of
it (the section on 'the armour of God') has already been
well explored by others, so we will not be looking at the
passage in any great detail. However, there are some
issues relating to the whole passage which we need to
consider if we are going to understand its comments on
praying.

This passage differs from the others in that, rather
than being a prayer, it is instruction about prayer. It is set
in a significant context, that of spiritual warfare. Paul
asserts that there are two ways in which we can build up
our strength – by using God's armour and through the
constant exercise of prayer. In doing so, we should try to
avoid being drawn into conflict with other human beings,
because it is Satan who is at work within all our human
struggles, failures and disappointments. Christians have a
cunning and vicious enemy, but Paul's main concern is to
show that we are well-equipped to fight him.

Having drawn our attention to the enemy, Paul exhorts
us to put on God's armour. He details its components –

the belt, breastplate, shoes, shield, helmet and sword – and he adds, 'Do all this in prayer, asking for God's help' (v 18). It may be that we operate in 'union with the Lord' through prayer and access his power through putting on his armour. Paul certainly understands prayer as a key to accessing God's power (1:16–19; 3:17–18,20). Indeed, he asks the Ephesians to pray for him so that he can fulfil his God-given calling (6:20). He is willing to part with one of his trusted colleagues, Tychicus, so that he can impart news of Paul's situation and thus provide the Ephesians with first-hand information and encouragement to pray. He did not see prayer, therefore, as the exclusive right of apostles. Prayer involved the whole church in praying as well as being blessed by prayer. Paul not only believed in prayer enough to pray for Christians everywhere; he believed in it enough to desire that they pray for him.

Paul's descriptions of how Christians are meant to live (4:1 – 6:9) may have left you feeling like an athlete who can just about cope with one event but who is suddenly told he has been entered for a decathlon! 'I'm meant to be fully involving myself in the life of the church, in spite of all the problems! I'm meant to be growing into a mature and sparkling Christian person, in spite of the counter pressures of my secular environment! To top it all, I need to live out my Christian values in my daily relationships, in spite of all kinds of corruption! I am certainly going to need to build up my stamina and skills!' Coming to this passage, after all that has gone before, it is natural to think that we need extraordinary strength to live ordinary Christian lives with integrity.

However, if we read verse 10 in the context of what follows, especially verse 12, our perspective alters. Now the kind of strength we need is 'spiritual'. This may seem immaterial, otherworldly, 'up there' rather than 'down here' in our ordinary experience. We may think, 'So *that's* what he means. We're to do it all by *prayer* – not by sheer effort!' After all, prayer is a 'spiritual' kind of process, isn't it? But I am not convinced that Paul is looking at two separate entities. He is not pointing us in two different directions, but towards two different ways of viewing the same reality.

One of my main frustrations in life concerns those so-called 'magic eye' pictures. Try as I will, and believe me I have tried as many methods as I have friends, I cannot see the hidden picture. People tell me how beautiful, startling, dynamic the hidden pictures are. I don't doubt that they are there, but the stubborn fact remains – I cannot see them. Even when there is a smaller one alongside the main picture, showing what is hidden, I have never managed to glimpse it, even for a second. I cannot get it to appear before my eyes. By the same analogy, Paul could see with equal ease two aspects of one reality – the surface picture and the hidden one – as he looked at the world of human experience. There is the more obvious physical aspect, the world of talking, relating, working, eating and drinking. But interwoven with this is the spiritual realm, where spiritual forces are at work.

When Peter dared to express the almost unthinkable – 'You are the Messiah, the Son of the living God' (Matt 16:16) – it is likely to have come as a bit of a surprise to the other disciples. He was probably articulating an impression that was already forming in their minds. They had seen the physical evidence – Jesus' authority, his power over demons and sickness, his miracles, even their own sense of awe – and could see that it pointed towards that conclusion. However, speaking it out in cold daylight may have seemed a little, well, shocking.

Jesus, however, could see what was happening at the other level, which we call 'spiritual'. Unlike me, he could see the hidden picture as well as the obvious one: 'This truth did not come to you from any human being, but it was given to you directly by my Father in heaven' (Matt 16:17). This is not to say that Peter didn't think and speak the words. They were *his* words; he was responsible for them. But another dimension was involved, which Jesus recognised to be the more significant one.

So Paul is looking to both the spiritual and physical realms when he says, 'build up your strength' (Eph 6:10). Both are at work in human affairs. Our thoughts, actions and emotions all have a spiritual dimension as well as a physical one. Thus heavenly authority and power shapes our human lives.

What happens when we review the components of God's armour as it integrates with prayer? We need *truth* to pray. We need to see people and situations for what they are, which includes seeing how they are subject to satanic pressures. In this way, we will not end up fighting against the people and the situations, but fighting for them. We need *righteousness*, both in the sense of being sure of our total acceptance by God (Rom 5:1–5; 8:14–17) and in the sense of our own integrity (James 5:16–18). Equally necessary is *faith* which like hope enables us to see beyond the circumstances that dampen our ability to pray, and *salvation* which gives us the confidence to pray and a focus for our praying. We have already spent some time seeing how the *word of God* facilitates and sustains prayer when both are serving God's Spirit.

Looked at in this way, it becomes plain that putting on God's armour and praying are inseparable activities. Without prayer, we won't be able to put on God's armour so as to protect ourselves effectively from the Devil's onslaughts, and the armour becomes a cumbersome uniform. Without the armour, our prayers will be weak and feeble. All the components of God's armour involve the interaction between the spiritual and physical dimension, both operating together to help us live faithfully for God in the world. Through prayer and through wearing God's armour, we can build up our strength in the Lord so that we genuinely reflect that we are part of God's new community. Together they provide us with the way to become stronger in God.

Paul rounds off his letter to the Ephesians with a challenge. Five times the summons comes to pray (6:18–20). We are being commanded to pray just as clearly as we have been urged to 'preserve the unity which the Spirit gives' or to 'be kind and tender-hearted to one another', or to 'submit yourselves to one another' by loving our spouses, respecting our parents and others in authority over us, and working cheerfully (4:3,32; 5:21; 6:7). It is part of the daily diet for the Christian life. Paul's challenge comes as the climax to his call 'to live a life that measures up to the standard God set when he called you' (4:1). We can do all the other things properly if we have sorted out our praying.

While it is inspiring to listen to a great pianist, those who would be pianists need to get involved in actually playing the piano themselves. In the same way, prayer is not just for the outstanding people of God like Paul; it is for ordinary people like us. Church members and ministers, those who struggle to control their tongues or their instincts, husbands and wives, parents and children, managers and workers are all called to pray. The effect of our prayers is much more to do with the God to whom we pray than with the people who are praying. So, having prayed passionately and movingly for God's hope, power and love to fill and enlarge the Ephesian Christians, Paul now calls them to get involved in actually praying.

Prayer ideas
Alone
1. Read Ephesians 6:10–20. Make a list of each section of God's armour and their equivalent in the Christian life.

God's armour	Equivalent in Christian life
Belt	*Truth*
Helmet	*Salvation*

Prayerfully reflect on which of these is a strength and which is a weakness for you. If it helps, mark each with 'S' (strength), or 'W' (weakness). Pray that you will use your strengths to help others, and that God will strengthen your weakness.

2. Thank God for the people in your church who are 'closest' to you – perhaps because they sit near you, or because you feel spiritually at ease with them or work together with them in the life of the church. Thank him for the way they protect you. Ask him to show you ways in which you can serve them.

3. 'For we are not fighting against human beings', but it can sometimes feel that way! Jesus tells us to bless those who persecute us and do good to those who hate us (Matt 5:43–44). One way to accomplish this is through prayer.

Think about the people you find difficult to relate to. Make a note of their names, and then write down next to each a couple of things that would bless them in some way. Every other day, pray that God will give you his love for these people and that you will see the good in them. On alternate days, pray that God will bless them and give them all they need, using your list of blessings as a guide.

Together

1. Having done No. 1 'Alone' above, share your weak points and pray for each other, that God will strengthen you.

2. Talk over some conflict situations and see if you can learn to see them at both the human and the spiritual level. Are there any 'techniques' you can share (remember the 'magic-eye' analogy)? We can always ask God for wisdom.

Pray about the spiritual issues that may impact the situations you noted.

3. Before you meet again, make notes on situations that you would like to understand at the two levels – spiritual and physical. Pray for these situations, then, when you meet, share your experiences. Ask God to give you growing discernment about them.

2 PRAY ALWAYS

> Do all this in prayer, asking for God's help. Pray on
> every occasion, as the Spirit leads. For this reason
> keep alert and never give up; pray always for all
> God's people. *(Ephesians 6:18)*

Two words, 'I will', seem so simple to say, but when
affirmed in the context of a wedding service they take on
a whole new significance. Indeed, few of us who have
been married for more than a few months, let alone years,
could say, 'I really understood what "I will" meant'. It is
the same with Paul's words, 'Pray always'. They sound so
simple but contain a range of meanings.

Pray regularly

First, 'pray always' can mean that we should pray regularly.
Don't allow anything or anyone to lull you into a false sense
of security or to pressurise prayer out of your life. Whether
relaxing on holiday or struggling to cope with the pressures
of life, prayer is such a priority we should never allow ourselves to be deprived of it. Prayer is never only 'for me'.
Even if I happen to be praying for apparently personal,
'first-person-singular' matters, others will be affected. In
prayer I am ensuring that my armour is useful and not
merely decorative, and my armour affects more than just
me. The shield of faith that covers me covers my friend too;

the sword of the Spirit not only keeps the enemy away from me but also from those nearest to me.

Anna was the kind of person you would probably hardly notice or, if you did, almost with a sense of pity! She was very old, 84 years to be precise. She had a face furrowed by her hard life. She did not get out and about at all. Indeed, she was no more noticeable to people than a lamp-post or stick of furniture – a familiar figure, always in the same place: 'She never left the Temple' (Luke 2:36–37). But to God, she was very special. She was chosen to be one of two people who would confirm to Joseph and Mary the significance of the child entrusted to them by God. What was it that prepared her for this sacred task? 'Day and night she worshipped God, fasting and praying.' Anna lived a life of disciplined devotion and consistent prayer. Undoubtedly, both she and her prayers were pleasing to God.

Now, I am not arguing here for some kind of legalistic ritual, that we must pray in the morning or evening or even both. However, establishing some kind of regular pattern for our prayer life can be of real help. Indeed, for most of us, the benefits probably outweigh the dangers of turning prayer into ritual. Jesus himself probably followed the Jewish pattern of praying morning, noon and night.[16] The depth of his prayer life suggests that there is some value in having some kind of routine. We can see for ourselves why this is. If we eat at regular times, if we establish a pattern for the intake of food, our bodies soon learn to let us know if, for any reason, we forget to eat. The normal routine acts as an in-built warning system. Similarly, if we establish a regular pattern for prayer, our spiritual being will let us know when it senses that we are neglecting to feed it with prayer.

Many people find that having a special room or a special posture can help them enter more quickly into the right attitude for prayer. Similarly, regular times for prayer can act as a 'trigger' to call us to prayer. This will alert us to Satan's wiles. We need to realise who it is who whispers that we don't have time to pray, who encourages us to 'lie in' rather than go to the morning prayer meeting, who probes our weaknesses to stop us praying.

Pray on every occasion

> [13] Are any of you in trouble? You should pray. Are any of you happy? You should sing praises. [14] Are any of you ill? You should send for the church elders, who will pray for them and rub olive oil on them in the name of the Lord. ... [16] So then, confess your sins to one another and pray for one another, so that you will be healed. The prayer of a good person has a powerful effect.' *(James 5:13–14,16)*

When everything is going well and life seems to be without pressure, when all seems under control and progressing smoothly, there is always the temptation to think we can manage without God. It is at times like these we need to pray.

When we are going through a difficult time, when every situation seems bad and without any possibility of improvement, it is at times like these we need to pray.

When life is one long, ordinary routine, when nothing spectacular is happening, that is when prayer is a vital ingredient.

In the times when life-changing decisions need to be made, or in the mundane minutiae of daily life, prayer is a gift from God. There is no situation that will not benefit from prayer.

Never give up

Often in Scripture we are encouraged to 'keep alert', 'to watch' as well as to pray. These phrases present two distinct but complementary pictures. The first is a military one, the obvious background in the Ephesian passage here. We all recognise that it is imperative for soldiers to keep alert. Frequently, the safety of colleagues as well as their own depends on the alertness of the sentries. The enemy will always seek to penetrate and destroy by attacking when we least expect. The other picture is that of the servant. Waiters at a banquet may appear to be standing around doing nothing for much of the time, but in fact, if they are doing their job properly, they are constantly vigilant so as to anticipate the needs of the guests or respond to any emergency that arises.

Both these pictures help us to grasp more clearly the kinds of alertness required for prayer. We need maximum awareness and sensitivity if we are to keep the enemy at bay and indeed penetrate his defences. We need an attitude of love and a servant-heart if we are to anticipate properly the needs of others and ensure they are met through prayer. We need a servant's eyes if we are to know what our Master desires and when it is the right time to act.

When John Wimber taught the thousands who attended his 'Equipping the Saints' conferences to 'pray with our eyes open', it seemed strange, almost improper to those of us who had been schooled to pray with our eyes closed. The practice of closing our eyes seemed a good one – it freed us from visual distractions, enabling us to focus all our attention on God. The problem for many of us is that it didn't work. Often closing our eyes meant our minds were freed to wander or to slumber!

Wimber, however, encouraged us to look at the person for whom we were praying. As we did so, we were then better able to seek to understand what God was doing for them and in them and, as a result, we could pray with more understanding. Prayer became more of a dynamic partnership with God. We were able to pray for longer and be more relaxed about it. If watching what God was doing for the other person was part of the prayer process, we did not need to feel guilty if we were not praying aloud. Many of us began to discover that the amount of words we used in no way equated with the level of God's response to our prayers. A few appropriate words often seemed to matter more than a torrent!

We can transfer these insights to more general praying. It helps to be aware of what is going on around us, what God is choosing to do in response to our prayers, and what Satan's counter-strategy is. So, whether we are praying for a national crisis or a family problem, the same principles apply. It requires spiritual discernment both to observe what is happening 'out there' and to understand what is going on 'up there'. When Daniel 'knelt down at the open windows and prayed' (Dan 6:10), he was able to look out on the pagan city and towards Jerusalem. In this way he could keep one eye on the problem and one eye on God. This, I believe, is the way to generate the spiritual energy to persevere in prayer.

Prayer is hard work. When is Satan most likely to make prayer seem hard and unrewarding? When we have almost reached the breakthrough point! For at that point he will have his last fling to stop us. When we are thinking, 'This is going nowhere', 'It doesn't make any difference', 'I'll do something else', it is then that we need to keep going and not give up. Pray with all perseverance. 'Let your hope keep you joyful, be patient in your troubles, and pray at all times' (Rom 12:12).

But persevering in prayer does not mean that we are trying to twist God's arm or insist that our will be done. Rather, it indicates that we are so deeply concerned to see God's kingdom come and his honour restored, we cannot rest until we see his answer come about. 'Prayer is not for getting man's will done in heaven; but for getting God's will done on earth' (Robert Law). This sometimes takes time, so we can and should go on praying until either God answers or the Spirit stops us.

George Müller, founder of several orphanages in Victorian England, was a man who knew how to persevere in prayer. The story goes that for about sixty years he prayed for two friends to come to faith. One came to faith just before he died, so he had the joy of seeing the fruit of his praying. But the other did not become a believer until after Müller's death. Prayer may take time and endurance, but it is never ever wasted.

Anna prayed in the Temple '*day and night*'. This is a Hebrew idiom, which means she was there all the time, praying constantly. This encouragement to 'never give up', to stand firm and hold our ground, appears to be a constant refrain in Paul's message to the churches (Rom 12:12; Eph 1:16; Phil 1:3–4; Col 1:3; 4:2; 1 Thess 3:10; 5:17; 2 Thess 1:11). How can it be done?

We need to recognise that prayer is 'the Christian's vital breath'. Just as we do not stop breathing when we go to sleep, neither do we need to stop praying because we are asleep – or because we are driving or writing or cooking or doing the housework. Prayer is a matter of our spirit crying to God or of God's Spirit crying through us. Such 'prayer without ceasing' will not happen automatically. It is something we must cultivate, as when a newborn baby first has to remember to breathe but then it quickly becomes an automatic response. One of my friends was surprised to discover that when he woke up he was pray-ing! Essentially, he is an activist, liking nothing better than to get his hands dirty sorting out a car engine or some other practical job. But he has allowed God access to his subconscious so that when his body or even his mind is occupied with other things, his spirit is in prayer. He has learnt to 'breathe prayer'.

What will help us get started? It is important to tell God this is what we want, then to invite him, through his Spirit, to bring it about. The journey of a thousand miles begins with the first step, so it helps to spend as much time in conscious prayer as we can. It is frightening how many hours most people spend watching television. For a week or a few weeks, why not have a 'fast' from TV and give the time to God? Alternatively, spend a day or a few days with God on a retreat.[17] We need to 'take every thought captive for Christ' and do what I call 'redeeming the time'. This involves finding opportunities to pray in all kinds of spare moments – the lost minutes waiting in queues, at the supermarket check-out or in doctors' surgeries. Instead of getting frustrated at having to wait, why not spend the time praying for the people having to wait with you, or for those who are keeping you waiting? So the fractious child, whose parent seems unable to control him, can become the focus for quiet prayer. When you lie awake at night, instead of being anxious that you are not sleeping, you can pray for others who cannot sleep – because of pain, or anxiety, or the cold because they are homeless; because they are looking after aged parents, or even because they are at work on our behalf. Or pray for those in other lands for whom it is now day.

A thousand possibilities soon emerge once you give this time to God. When you watch television, during the advertising slot, instead of letting yourself be drip-fed consumerism gone mad, you could use the time to pray. Turn down the sound, close your eyes and pray, perhaps using the programmes you are watching to give you direction. When you read the papers or listen to the news on the radio, turn each topic into prayer.

Walking offers other opportunities. Whether you are taking the dog across the park or the children to school, the sounds, sights and smells that drift towards you, everyday or unusual objects, can become stimuli to prayer. One way to grow into this kind of praying on the move is to take part in a prayer walk.[18] As the pastor of a church, I have often found that people whom I did not consider especially 'prayerful' eagerly took part in this kind of prayer and grew in faith as a result. What you are doing as you develop this God-ward tendency in all your life is increasing your capacity to 'pray without ceasing'. You will soon find that your subconscious is God's territory, with all the tremendous benefits that flow out of this.

We can also gain comfort from realising that that there is a corporate component to this kind of praying. In some larger churches, or with some inter-church prayer chains, it is an effective strategy to set up a round-the-clock prayer-watch. In Kensington Temple in London, for instance, they have such a large group of intercessors there is at least one person praying throughout every hour of every week. Even if smaller fellowships cannot manage this, it may well be possible to organise a day or two at a time to give thanks or pray for a need. Churches could link up with one another and ensure that their neighbourhood or their church denomination has this kind of total prayer cover.

The roof of a house is made up of hundreds of tiles, each one quite small. On their own they would not keep the occupants of the house dry. Together and because they interlock they can offer real protection. If one or two tiles are blown off by the wind, then the rain can get in and cause damage which may affect the whole house. There is clearly a sense in which we should seek to link 'tiles of prayer' to provide a cover for organisations and situations.

The result of such prayer without ceasing is hard to overestimate, as the following 'classic' prayer story illustrates. In 1727 the Herrnhut community, established five years earlier by the then twenty-one-year-old Count Zinzendorf, started a prayer vigil that covered every hour for one hundred years. Such praying led first to the stabilisation and renewal of the community. Then the community became part of the answer to its own prayers that God would revive the church and meet the needs of the world. Within a hundred years the community had sent over two thousand missionaries to Europe, the West Indies, Ceylon, South Africa and India. This began, let us not forget, with one man's commitment to God, amplified by the corporate and continuous praying of his fellow pray-ers.

To summarise then, the phrase 'Pray always' can mean 'pray regularly' at specific times. It can mean 'pray in every kind of situation or context'. Finally, it can mean 'pray without ceasing'. Such simple words, such a lifetime's challenge. Maybe we need to respond 'I will'!

Sometimes life is so hectic we don't have a moment to spare. Sometimes it seems as though there is nothing going on at all. But at all times prayer has a real place. If we are too busy to pray, we are too busy. If we have nothing to do, we can soon be busy doing nothing but pray. If occasionally we start to think, 'This is no time for prayer', then we can remind ourselves of Jesus who, having emptied himself and endured the cross, now commits his life in eternity to one thing – prayer for us.

> And so he is able, now and always, to save those who come to God through him, because he lives for ever to plead with God for them. *(Hebrews 7:25)*

Prayer ideas
Alone

1. It can be liberating to realise that God has made us all different. Some people are *planners* (they like to make lists, put things away in one place; they dislike the unexpected), while others are more *spontaneous* (they like to just get on and do things, sort things any old how, welcome disruptions; they dislike routine). Which are you? Or are you somewhere in between (sometimes spontaneous, other times more organised). Mark where you think you are on the following chart.

Planner									Spontaneous	
5	4	3	2	1	O	1	2	3	4	5

Think about two of your friends. Where would you put them? How do you think this might affect the way they enjoy praying? Thank God for the way he has made each of you.

2. Set aside three ten-minute slots in your day and use them for prayer. Perhaps using a prayer liturgy or a piece of scripture will help, or you could work out a pattern of your own for each one.

- Morning – for prayer about 'new beginnings': any new projects or relationships you are embarking on, or old ones you want a new perspective on.

- Noon – for prayer about work, colleagues.

- Evening – for prayer about rest, committing people and situations to God.

3. Think over the events of today, or the last week. Can you identify times or situations that caused you frustration? Are there activities that occupy your hands but leave your mind free to roam? Why not make use of these as opportunities for prayer? Try keeping a journal about your day and how you have brought God into these times. After a few weeks, review whether learning to 'redeem this time' has helped you.

4. One way to help yourself 'pray without ceasing' is to find a 'trigger' – a short phrase such as 'Jesus, Lamb of God, who takes away the sin of the world, have mercy on us'; a verse from a Christian song; a picture; or an object such as a small wooden cross or pebble in your pocket. Use your 'trigger' as often as you can to prompt you to pray, until prayer becomes an 'automatic response'.

Together

1. Do you know people in your church or family who are 'Annas'? Share with each other what you know about such people and thank God for them. If you were God, why do you think they would be special to you? Can you encourage the 'Annas' you have in your church? How will you do this?

2. One way to build up perseverance in prayer is to join with others in making a kind of covenant. When we are discouraged, they will help us to continue or even keep prayer going when we give up for a time. Then we can return to the battlefield refreshed.

3. Agree together that you will seek to cover an event or need with continuous prayer. Possibilities include weddings, medical operations, church missions or critical decisions that need to be taken in the church or in wider society. Work out how you will recruit people to pray, allocate time-slots, provide information, arrange for feedback and thank people afterwards. When you have done this, review your strategy together. What worked/didn't work? Could anything be improved?

4. Share any knowledge you have of other churches and the way they organise their corporate prayer life. If you sense that you are short on information, write to people you know in other churches, or visit them, to find out how they pray. When you have done this, assess if they have any practical ideas that might work in your church. You may wish to pilot these in your group.

3 FOR ALL GOD'S PEOPLE

¹⁸ ...pray always for all God's people. ¹⁹ And pray also for me, that God will give me a message when I am ready to speak, so that I may speak boldly and make known the gospel's secret. ²⁰ For the sake of this gospel I am an ambassador, though now I am in prison. Pray that I may be bold in speaking about the gospel as I should. *(Ephesians 6:18–20)*

One of the joys to look forward to in heaven is the diversity we will find there: 'an enormous crowd ... from every race, tribe, nation, and language' (Rev 7:9–12). This huge body of God's people surrounds his throne, calling out his praises 'in a loud voice'. Prayer, then, is the music of our spirits playing in concert. Though it has many languages and is found in many different human contexts, it embraces all who are part of God's family. Wherever we live and whatever our ethnic background, we are part of the Body of Christ. In him, the differences between us are transcended (Eph 2:19; 4:3–4). We are committed to respect and care for others in the church (1 Cor 12–14), and prayer plays a crucial role in achieving this.

So we are called to pray for countless millions! Why should we do this? And how can we avoid being overwhelmed? Prayer is a priceless gift, a matchless opportunity. The future of the world is in God's hands, and that future is bound up with the future of his people (Rom 8:18–22). Prayer transforms people, pressures, problems, situations and relationships. It has unlimited power because its only limit is an infinite God. So in praying for God's people we will be participating with him in fulfilling his purpose for the world.

Prayer builds relationships. Positive relationships help motivate us to pray. When we pray *for* people as well as *with* them, relationships are formed, developed and strengthened. Prayer is itself a form of relationship. It includes thanking God for those we are praying for, forgiving them (or asking their forgiveness), seeking to understand their needs, desiring their well-being and their place in the purposes of God, as well as interceding directly for them. Through prayer, our lives become interlocked.

Praying for all God's people develops those who pray. Prayer for those we know builds our faith as we see God bring blessing into their lives. Meanwhile, prayer for those further afield helps build our stamina for the work of the kingdom and increases our awareness of the vastness of God's purposes.

Finally, praying for all God's people saves us from becoming egocentric or insular. We are all inclined to relate well to those we like. Becoming caught up with others helps us to appreciate more fully the intricacies of the whole Body of Christ. In doing so, we begin to understand and experience the purposes of God. We become more generous with our money and our time. We grow in our desire to witness and gain a greater sense of the dynamics of the Great Commission, upon whose fulfillment depends the return of Christ (Matt 24:14). In other words, praying for all God's people promotes the health of the Body of Christ, individually and corporately.

Jesus commissioned his disciples to witness for him in 'Jerusalem, in all Judea and Samaria, and to the ends of the earth' (Acts 1:8). This provides us with a good model for our own prayers: we can begin where we are, the people and situations we are involved with, and move out from there. As we do, we will find that our prayers for our own arena will help us know how to pray for the wider world.

Do we need to restrict our prayers to our time? There were saints before us and there will be saints after us. I believe that prayer for all God's people must include those who are, from our perspective, dead – 'this large crowd of witnesses round us' (Heb 12:1). I believe we can pray meaningfully for them, giving thanks to God for them just as fully and as freely as for those who are alive. Whether the focus of our prayers is a great Christian like Paul or someone in our own family; whether they are recently dead or have been for a thousand years, they are part of the fullness of God's gift too. Second, if we need to, we can offer forgiveness to them through God. Sometimes death robs us of the opportunity to establish harmonious relationships. We may need to ask God to bring his peace into such a relationship. Equally, as we confess our sins to God, we can also ask that he forgive us for sins we may have committed against them. Such prayers will give us a growing appreciation of the saints who have gone before us and the inheritance they have handed on to us.

And what about coming generations? Revelation 8:1–5 seems to suggest that God gathers together the prayers of his people, implying that prayers offered now can be applied in the future. It seems sensible to me, therefore, that we can pray for those who are not yet born. If our prayers can transcend distance, surely they can transcend time?

I first shared my thoughts on this issue at the Santa Clara Valley Vineyard Fellowship. To illustrate my point, I shared with them the example of Hudson Taylor, the great pioneer missionary to China, who committed himself to pray for the fourth generation of his family – not only that they would become Christians but that they would become Christian leaders. As is well known, generation after generation fulfilled the prayers of the man who said he did not have great faith in God but had faith in a great God.

The lady whose invitation had taken me to California interrupted me at this point. In semi-disbelief, she said, 'But *I* am one of that fourth generation...' It was one of those 'so much more' moments that Paul promises us in Ephesians 3:20. We felt that we were connected – that faithful servant of God, this lady and I – in a link that transcended time and space.

I am sure that I too have benefited from the prayers of many who, whether they knew me well or not, have yet blessed me with their prayers. I hope that others as yet unborn will live to thank God for our faithfulness.

'Pray also for me'

Paul's prayers are both majestic and intimate: he knows God's awesome power yet enjoys a close relationship with God. In the new churches across the Mediterranean, in Ephesus and elsewhere, were people struggling with their pagan background and immorality, quarrelling among themselves, getting their faith all wrong. Yet Paul, this great prayer warrior, does not disdain their prayers. 'Pray for me,' he asks them time and again. We too should be willing to ask others to pray for us, whoever we are. And we should remember to pray for others, especially those in leadership.

> [1] First of all, then, I urge that petitions, prayers requests, and thanksgivings be offered to God for all people; [2] for kings and all others who are in authority, that we may live a quiet and peaceful life with all reverence towards God and with proper conduct. [3] This is good and it pleases God our Saviour, [4] who wants everyone to be saved and to come to know the truth. *(1 Timothy 2:1–4)*

In his book, *Good Morning Disciple*, Vic Jackopson, makes this observation:

> In his book *Perestroika*, Mikhail Gorbachov suddenly springs to life, when he quotes from a number of letters sent to him by well-wishers. One, which cheered my heart, came from V. A. Brikovskis who encouraged her leader like this: 'Every Sunday I go to church and pray that God refrain from punishing the world for our sins. I know you are an atheist, but through your efforts you have shown that some believers have something to learn from you. I want you to know that every Sunday I am in church from nine a.m. to one p.m. praying for you and your family' ... Even the unbeliever, in my experience, is most appreciative when he knows that someone is praying for him.

As Christians, we are not only to respect and obey those in authority, we are to pray positively for them. We can base our prayers on the injunction from the prophet Micah: 'the Lord has told us what is good. What he requires of us is this: to do what is just, to show constant love, and to live in humble fellowship with our God' (Micah 6:8). On this basis, we can pray that our leaders govern justly, generously and sensitively. And, if we are to pray for all leaders, how much more our Christian leaders, whether their ministry is in the church or in the world. If we want effective leadership, we need to ask God for it and seek for ways in which we might contribute towards bringing it about. Prayer is fundamental if leadership is to be effective, if the flock is to be built up, if future leaders are to emerge.

One factor that may well surprise many Christian leaders is that often their flock don't think they need prayer! They perceive their leaders to be already super-spiritual, powerful, constantly in touch with God, fully gifted and beyond contradiction. Those of us in positions of leadership would probably be amazed by this perception. We are more likely to feel like Paul – 'the chief of sinners'! Leaders need to foster prayer for themselves by asking for it. We need to encourage people to pray for us so that they see leadership as something they are involved in, too. Then they will realise that it is as much their responsibility to establish effective leadership as it is the leader's.

Asking for prayer gives a leader the opportunity to explain what is going on not only in his or her life but in the life of the entire group. He can bring up vital issues and provide the relevant information that serves as the fuel for prayer. Paul did this by sending people like Tychicus to Ephesus to report personally. When this wasn't possible, he sent letters. Even when leaders are in a settled and permanent ministry, they should constantly inform those under them about their work, plans, successes, failures, joys and worries. Providing such information may take time, energy, organisation and money, but it enables the group to pray effectively and gives them a sense of vision and purpose. I am convinced that it is prayer which generates the creative response, the unexpected breakthrough.

Those of us who are followers may be tempted to criticise our leaders, but we need to turn such criticisms into positive prayer. We can praise God that he has appointed them for the growth of his Body, and give thanks for what is good and godly in their life. We may also need to pray for forgiveness on our part. Thus we can turn Satan's strategy back on him in prayer. Clearly this is much easier when leaders follow Paul's pattern and ask for prayer. If they don't, then maybe we can make this our first priority for them.

If Paul is advocating prayer for all the saints, then presumably it is sensible for all the saints to ask for prayer, whether we are in leadership or not. Those in leadership may have the privilege of asking others for prayer, but they in turn need to pray for those under them. Even

Jesus saw the necessity of praying for his disciples (John 17). Such prayer will deepen our sense of community, which is one of the vital gifts the church has to offer to modern society. We could follow Micah's advice and ask for prayer that we do what is just, show constant love, and live in humble fellowship with our God.

Some people think they can cope without prayer. However, it is important to remember that we are not meant to be spiritual 'Lone Rangers'. Asking for prayer serves to remind us that, individually, we are part of the Body of Christ. We can't do anything without our Head and we can't do much without the rest of the Body (1 Cor 12). Without God we are helpless, and we need others to pray for us so that we are empowered to live for Christ and be his faithful witnesses, especially in presenting the gospel (Eph 6:20).

As we read the account of Paul's missionary journeys in Acts, and follow his correspondence, the last thing most of us would have expected was that he needed prayer for boldness in his presentation of the gospel. Whether debating with learned philosophers in Athens, facing a hostile mob in Ephesus, dealing with dangerous criminals in Philippi, or coping with an over-enthusiastic crowd in Lystra, he always seems confident, composed and compelling in his expression of the Good News of Jesus. Neither weariness nor the strength of opposition seem to faze him in the slightest. But it often is the case that at the very place where a person appears strong and extraordinarily successful is the place where he or she struggles and feels vulnerable:

> ...we who have this spiritual treasure are like
> common clay pots, in order to show that the supreme
> power belongs to God, not to us. *(2 Corinthians 4:7)*

Asking for prayer requires that we let people nearer to our heart than we may find comfortable. It requires a degree of honesty with our own feelings. But such vulnerability allows God to build us together into a living wall instead of remaining a disjointed pile of bricks.

We should not hesitate, then, to seek the prayer support of others. We need never be ashamed to say, 'Pray for me'. As we see the prayers of others for us answered, we will experience real joy. As we see our prayers answered in the lives of others, we will share in God's victory over sin and death. With the power of prayer behind us, we will find that God accomplishes for us far more than we ever dared to imagine.

Prayer ideas
Alone

1. Pay a visit to a travel agent and select brochures from a few countries. Then go to the library and borrow books about two or three countries that appeal to you. Ask God to show you the needs of the people in those countries. Discover what you can about the state of the church there. Gradually, your concern for those countries will grow and you can build your prayers.

2. Find out where some major event will be taking place, such as a world summit or the Olympic Games. Get as much information as you can and start praying. There will always be some form of Christian presence at such events. Support them by 'building a highway for God' through your prayers.

3. Think of a leader you know either personally or from the news, from each of the following categories: church, business, industry, local government, news media, science, politics (national and international), arts and music, sport. Find out as much as you can about them, their concerns and what they will be doing over the following weeks or months. Perhaps you could stick a photo of them up on a pinboard or in a scrapbook. You might even write to them and let them know you are praying for them! Then support them in prayer. Look out for news items about them to keep you up to date with what's happening in their lives. Thank God for them. Pray for them and their families, asking that they will contribute to the well-being of the community they serve, and that they will live with integrity. Whether they are Christians or not, pray that God will use what they do to progress the gospel.

4. Make a list of the leaders in your church. How much time do you spend praying for them? Imagine that each one is asking for prayer. Against the name of each, write what you think they would ask you to pray for – their family, their ministry, their Christian growth. Then spend time praying for them. When you have opportunity, find out whether or not your prayers have been answered. Keep asking God to give you further insight into their real needs: remember – as in Paul's case, these might surprise you.

5. Whether you have leadership responsibilities or not, have you asked others to pray for you? You can do this in a number of ways – for example, talking or writing to friends; holding a special prayer supper, breakfast or bar-becue; producing a monthly prayer diary or annual prayer card. See how creative you can be. Meet regularly with those praying for you and ask them whether you are giv-ing them enough of the right kind of information to stim-ulate their continued support. Let them know how much you appreciate their prayers, and talk over together what would help them keep going.

Together

1. As a group, review the ways in which your church or fellowship prays 'for all God's people'. Are there some people or groups who are often overlooked? Can you find ways to stimulate prayer for them? Determine who they are and how you can pray for them.

2. Give each group member the task of finding out about one church or fellowship in the place where they will spend their holidays. They could bring back the magazines of churches they have visited, explore web sites, share stories about people they met. They could also bring photographs of the places they visited (and food?) to share with the group. Spend time in prayer together. Encourage each person to write to their 'holiday' church to let them know they have been prayed for and to ask for more prayer requests. Who knows where this adventure will lead, how many strong relationships will be forged?

3. As a group, 'adopt' a country. Find out all you can about it and about the Christians there, perhaps using some of the suggestions in this chapter. See if your leaders would welcome some input about this country and its needs in a service or through the church magazine. Better still, why not put on an evening to celebrate that country's food and culture?

4. Construct a church 'family tree' or a 'prayer photo album' of people who have served in the church in the past, who are now dead. Use this to stimulate your thanksgiving. You may discover that church members today were significantly affected by these earlier members. In such cases, your prayers will naturally focus on them, too – that they will benefit fully from their inheritance.

5. Talk over in your group whether or not you find it easy to ask others to pray for you. Is it easier to ask for prayer for group concerns rather than personal ones? If you find it difficult to ask for prayer, consider booking time with someone who can act as a pastor-counsellor to you and prayerfully work out why this is. Think what strategies you can develop (individually and as a group) to improve the situation.

6. Resolve to pray for leaders you know, either from your church, in your workplace, maybe even parents. Write their names, their roles and their prayer needs on separate sheets of paper. Each group member commits to pray for one person until the group next meets. Then they can each pray for someone different.

Alternatively, individuals can talk about a local or national leader in politics or business who matters to them. Pray for that person, then move on to pray for someone else's leader.

Note

This chapter may have prompted you to think about praying for or with your family. If so, a helpful, positive and enjoyable book on the subject is *And all the Children said, 'Amen'* by Ian Knox (Scripture Union, 1994).

Conclusion: Ephesians 3:20-21
SO MUCH MORE

Our adventure of prayer through Ephesians is almost at an end, but the real adventure is only now beginning. Before I leave you to embark on your own adventure, let's explore Ephesians 3:20–21 together, to give us a final impetus to pray.

> 20 To him who by means of his power working in us is able to do so much more than we can ever ask for, or even think of: 21 to God be the glory in the church and in Christ Jesus for all time, for ever and ever! Amen. *(Ephesians 3:20–21)*

These verses have been a constant source of energy and power to me as, over the last few years, my ministry has taken me up and down the UK and across the world. I have lived these verses. Whenever I have visited a new church, met the leadership team of an organisation, or been part of a committee for evangelism, this has been my prayer: 'Help me to see your "so much more"!' So often he has. I never know when or how God is going to surprise me with his bonus, but it happens all the time. These verses have become central for my life.

They also seem central to Ephesians, too. They are like the hinges on which the door turns. Ephesians 1–3 tells us of all that God has done for us; Ephesians 4–6 tells us of all that should follow in our Christian life as a consequence of

God's great act of salvation. These verses, 3:20–21, occupy a pivotal position. Paul tells us that God can do 'so much more than we can ever ask for'. Immediately this poses the question 'How much is so much more?'

An evangelist friend of mine tells how he was once travelling back from America. In the seat next to him on the aeroplane was a Texan who was clearly of the 'larger than life' variety. This man wanted to know what my friend was doing and who he was working for. My friend did not want to be 'outgunned' and he also wanted to create an opportunity to share the gospel! So he invited the Texan to guess who he worked for. To help him, he said he would give him a clue: 'The organisation I work for is bigger than yours.'

The Texan went through all the oil companies. The evangelist assured him his boss was bigger! Then he went through all the UK companies – then the Japanese, then the multinationals. But none of them, my friend said, matched the one he works for. In the end the Texan gave up. 'OK, I'll tell you,' the evangelist said. 'I work for the one who owns the world, I work for God and this is what I do...'

No matter how big our perspectives or our prayers, 'the world and all that is in it belong to the Lord' (Psalm 24:1). Paul knew that God is much bigger than his world. He knew the greatness of God's purpose; he knew the greatness of God's plans for his people (Eph 1:10–11; 2:19–22; 4:13; Col 1:15–23). So he prayed big prayers, the prayers of someone who understood the mighty power of his God, and the vastness of his compassion and lovingkindness.

When my daughter was about six, as Christmas began to approach (it was the beginning of November!), Hannah became very excited at the prospect of new toys. One night we wondered how we would cope for that evening, let alone the next two months. In the end, to help calm her down, she was sent to bed with a catalogue from the local store and told to look through it and write her list. We thought the ploy had worked and that she must have gone to sleep, for all went quiet. Then suddenly she reappeared, her face alight, with a list of a hundred or so things she wanted for Christmas in her hand. We told her there was no way she could possibly expect to get all these things – could she please cut the list down.

'But this already is my urgent list,' she said.

'Sorry, but can we have your "very urgent" list?'

Even her 'very urgent' list was more than we could manage!

However, according to Paul, we don't need to cut down our list for God. Rather, we need to expand it! We will never exhaust his resources or resourcefulness. So expand your list, write it down, pray it out, whatever there is, there is still more to come from God. *He is able* to do more.

> His ability is beyond even our imagination! Let us stretch our imaginations to the utmost. What is it possible for us to become? And when our imagination has almost wearied itself in the effort to conceive, it is 'above all we can think of' ... the power of Christ, like the love of Christ is beyond human understanding or measurement. It is like trying to measure the distance to the edge of the galaxy with a ruler! *(J H Jowett)* [19]

What we can only dream of, God can do. He is the one who can turn our dreams into his realities, by means of his power, the Holy Spirit working in us. This is the same Spirit responsible for creation, revelation and resurrection (Eph 1:19–20; 3:16). And we have a part to play in the fulfilling of our kingdom dreams. We are the chosen medium, as the electricity wires are the medium for the power station's energy to flow.

On the way to seeing our dreams fulfilled, we will almost certainly be significantly changed ourselves. God's power is able to make those who are 'spiritually dead' powerfully alive. He can make those who live in darkness

the children of the light. He can make those who are ene-
mies and aliens one in Christ. He can turn fatigue into
fighting fitness, sinners into saints, ordinary churches
into communities that throb with victory and vitality. He
can bring revival sweeping through his church, the city,
the country, the world. But we must let him make the connection that empowers us.

In January 1993, a huge oil tanker, several hundred feet
long, lost power and slowly started to drift towards the
coast of Scotland, pulled by the tidal flow and by ever-
increasing winds which were mounting to gale force. All
the crew were lifted off, but the tanker continued heading
remorselessly for the coast. Violent waves drove it onto
the rocks, disgorging its dark cargo of crude oil over the
beautiful coastlands, polluting and disfiguring them.
Experts will always disagree about the real cause and the
long-term consequences of the accident. But a senior pilot
on one of the tugs involved in the attempted rescue said
that the greatest tragedy was that the whole incident
could have been avoided. If just one person had stayed on
board, the whole boat could have been rescued and disaster averted, because the tug could have fixed a line to
the helpless tanker and towed it out of danger. But there
was no one on board.

Those who pray will often be like the person who
stayed on board and changed the whole situation. Is there
anyone there to receive the line? God can do so much
more than we can imagine, but have we moved too soon
from the point of rescue? His 'so much more' is effected
by his power working in us, and we are not always willing
or able to let him do in us what needs to be done.
Sometimes we expect him to work with us, when the way
to victory is that we work with him. God cannot change.
We must be the ones to change, lining up our lives with
his purposes, willing to surrender our wills to his. It's no
good saying, 'Surely it's up to God to move!'

Often we feel that we cannot be good enough for God.

We are all too aware of our weakness and failure. Jennifer Rees Larcombe comes from a well-known Christian family. She was active in God's service, and had her own delightful and demanding family to occupy her time and attention. Then encephalitis (inflammation of the brain, meninges and nerves) struck. It left her in a wheelchair, dependent on others for most aspects of living, robbed of her ability to function fully as a mother. Everything medically and spiritually was tried.

Since Jennifer was well-known in Christian circles, people with 'healing ministries' found their way to her. She reached the stage, however, where she felt that God was not going to bring healing. During this period of several years she lived a remarkable Christian life, giving testimony to her faith in God through her weakness and inability. Then God gave her a promise that one day things would change. It was a promise she hardly dare hang on to, lest it was simply yet more wishful thinking. But it turned out to be a valid promise from God. And Wendy, the person God chose to be his instrument for healing, had only been a Christian a few months. Jennifer had a difficult time persuading Wendy to pray for her – Wendy felt she wasn't good enough and hardly knew how to pray. But God fulfilled his promise to Jennifer in a remarkable way, revealing his glory in the church. Her experience demonstrates his power to transform, forgive and recreate the most unlikely people through the most unlikely people![20]

In the church, God has brought us the knowledge of his glory, some revelation of himself (2 Cor 4:6). He has enabled us to reflect this glory to others; indeed we are being transformed into his glory (2 Cor 3:18). We respond to him in prayer (Eph 6:10–20). Yet it is God's gift. All the glory returns ultimately to him. This means that when anyone becomes a Christian, the glory is God's. When anyone overcomes temptation, the glory is God's. When anyone is helped, healed or comforted, the glory is God's.

When anyone gives their life in martyrdom, the glory is God's. When anyone sacrificially devotes themselves to serving others, the glory is God's. The church is called to do its utmost to ensure that both believers and unbelievers alike know that the glory, praise and adoration are God's. Our *raison d'être* is to ensure that he receives all the honour, that it is his light and love that people sense, not our achievements. 'Let us praise his glory' (1:1–14).

I take no pleasure in seeing the church criticised or demeaned. I long for the church, in all its manifestations, to be honoured not because of its splendid architecture, be it ancient or modern; nor because of its music or liturgy, be it traditional or spontaneous; nor because of its fellowship or its organisation; but because in it all there is an unavoidable sense that 'God is here and he is wonderful'. I am sure that the paradox is, the more the church becomes the centre for the pure glory of God, the more it becomes glorious too! 'To God be glory in the church and in Christ Jesus.'

Christ is God's glory (John 1:14; 17:5; Col 1:15), yet he always gave glory to God, always did what the Father wanted, always pointed to the Father. The whole human history of Jesus – his birth, his growing, his living, his ministry, his dying – was aimed at giving glory to God and to call others to do likewise. The Head is still trying to get the Body to do the same. This will come about as we pray in faith, receiving the 'so much more' and delighting to share this with others. This is the eternal calling of the church. What is it that we see when God draws back the curtain separating time and eternity? It is the church giving glory to the Father through its life and its praise:

> 7 The Lamb went and took the scroll from the right hand of the one who sits on the throne.
> 8 As he did so, the four living creatures and the twenty-four elders fell down before the Lamb. Each had a harp and gold bowls filled with incense, which are the prayers of God's people. 9 They sang a new song:

'You are worthy to take the scroll
   and to break open its seals.
For you were killed, and by your sacrificial death
            you bought for God
   people from every tribe, language, nation, and race.
10 You have made them a kingdom of priests to
            serve our God,
   and they shall rule on earth.'
11 Again I looked, and I heard angels, thousands
and millions of them! They stood round the throne,
the four living creatures, and the elders, 12 and sang
in a loud voice:
   'The Lamb who was killed is worthy
      to receive power, wealth, wisdom, and strength,
      honour, glory, and praise!'
13 And I heard every creature in heaven, on earth,
in the world below, and in the sea – all living beings
in the universe – and they were singing:
   'To him who sits on the throne and to the Lamb,
      be praise and honour, glory and might,
      for ever and ever!'
14 The four living creatures answered, 'Amen!' And
the elders fell down and worshipped.
(Revelation 5:7–14)

'Man's chief end is to glorify God and enjoy him for ever'
(Westminster Catechism). Unfortunately many if not most
of us have forgotten this fundamental truth:

Adam had a fall and he received a terrible bump;
involved with him in the catastrophe was Eve, his
wife. Then when they tried to shake the fog out of
their minds, looking at each other, they realized that
they no longer knew who they were, and they did not
know the purpose of their existence. Ever since that
time, men and women, alienated from God and trying
to exist on a sick fallen planet have been pleading, 'I
don't even know why I was born!' *(W Tozer)* [21]

Through prayer, we can rediscover the answer. As God gives more than we can imagine, we will know that we have an infinite loving Father. We will see his glory and declare his glory in the church. So we need to go on asking, knowing that God can and will do far more than we ask. We need to go on dreaming, knowing that God is far bigger than our dreams. We need to go on praising, proclaiming the wonder and glory of this God who delights to answer our prayers. As we do so, the greatest prayer of the human heart will be answered: 'Tell me who I am.'

God's answer far exceeds our wildest dreams. Amazingly, we discover that we are made for intimacy and eternal life with God (Eph 1:5,12). To call you into this adventure, so that you may enjoy him more, is why this book was written. I pray that now you have read it, you will go away and live it, too.

Appendix
'DO ALL THIS IN PRAYER'

One of the inherent features of life today in the relatively wealthy West is the plethora of things available for us to choose from. Of nothing else is this more true than our choice of food. The traditional English roast, Chinese take-away, Indian, Italian, Mexican, Korean, Thai, Caribbean, American fast-food, health foods – the list grows monthly. We don't need all this variety to survive, yet this wide choice does add to our enjoyment of life – though it may take some of us a while to get round to try-ing the latest possibility...

The same is true of prayer. We are fortunate in that we can select from a wide range of traditions and styles. Sooner or later we will probably encounter and be enriched by forms of prayer which at first seem strange to us. People from 'liturgical' churches can enjoy (or endure!) the flexibility of 'spontaneous' prayers. Those who have become used to spontaneity can be blessed by the beauty of the liturgical traditions.

What is undeniable is that God loves his children to pray. There is no situation we cannot bring to him, noth-ing that can prevent us coming to him. And we should 'do all this in prayer, asking for God's help ... as the Spirit leads' (Eph 6:18). We can pray on our own, in pairs, in small groups or in thousands. We can pray for things; we can pray against things; we can pray the scriptures; we can sing our prayers. We can pray in a circle with arms around one another...

Although most of us will welcome such a variety of styles and traditions, what ultimately matters is that our 'prayer menu' contains a healthy balance of all the ingredients we really need to keep our prayer life growing and interesting. There is, fortunately, one significant difference between food and prayer – unlike food, it is difficult to overindulge in prayer. Dieting is rarely needed. What a relief!

Some people find an acrostic helps them to keep a balance in their prayers. ACTS is a favourite one:

- Adoration
- Confession
- Thanksgiving
- Supplication

I prefer a simpler one which correlates with the 'food' illustration given above (this is used by Evangelism Explosion):

- Forgiveness
- Asking
- Thanksgiving

Initially, this may seem to lack the primary focus on God that the praise and adoration of ACTS has. A good way to think of praise in this framework is to see it as the delicious fragrance from the kitchen which increases our appetite!

Some will find it helpful to follow the pattern of The Lord's Prayer, which is, more accurately, 'The Disciple's Prayer'. A simple outline based on this prayer looks like this:

- Focus on God ('Our Father in heaven...').
- Commitment to God ('your kingdom come...').
- Requests for our human needs ('Give us today our daily bread...').
- Relationships ('Forgive us our debts [sins]...').
- Spiritual protection ('And lead us not into temptation...').
- Surrender to God ('Yours is the kingdom...').

Any such pattern will help to ensure that we have a balanced diet for prayer. Exploring the variety of prayer will enhance our appetite enormously.

Different kinds of prayers

A whole book could probably be written on the variety of prayers available. A visit to your local Christian bookshop should provide you with examples of most types. While this is not the primary purpose of this book, it is worthwhile exploring at least some of them.

Liturgical prayers

Prayers used in the set liturgies of the traditional churches are very good at helping us sense that we are part of the 'communion of the saints'. As we recollect when and how these prayers have been used over the centuries, we will gain a sense that we are praying as the body of Christ, even when we are on our own. Normally, these prayers contain a very balanced menu. However, their formality may mean that we don't 'own them' very deeply. Think of the people across the centuries who have used the same prayers, and those across the world who still do. Thank God for them.

Written prayers

There are hundreds of books available of prayers, ancient and modern, that can help put into words what we may find hard to say. Because these prayers have been carefully composed by deeply spiritual people, there is often a wholesomeness about them that spontaneous prayers may lack. Again, there is the danger that we use them too casually and they become a substitute for prayer rather than a means of praying. Of course, we can write our own prayers, and this process may lead us to ponder on our praying for longer. Just writing a prayer is itself a form of praying.

Why not visit your local library or Christian bookshop and choose a varied selection of books on prayer?

Experiment with other people's prayers. It is important to remember that there is a vast difference between reading prayers out loud and praying them. It could be a profitable exercise to compile your own anthology of prayers for all kinds of situations and people. Alternatively, you may find a few styles helpful and use them as a basis from which to write your own prayers for different sets of circumstances.

Spontaneous prayers

These prayers flow out of the heart as well as the mind, emanating from our child-father relationship with God. Such prayers are capable of expressing genuine feeling and deep commitment, and have a homely, personal quality to them. However, we must guard against their becoming trite, selfish and senseless.

Silent prayers

We don't necessarily need to speak words out loud to God – he reads our minds and hearts, and searches our spirits. Sometimes it is a relief not to have to find words, which are never entirely adequate and can sometimes distract us from God or even be used as a defence against him.

Shout!

Sometimes it is good to shout, for example, 'Hallelujah!' or 'Amen!' Used in a corporate context, shouting our praise helps to increase our sense of participation. It can also generate a sense of spiritual affirmation. We must beware, however, that we don't confuse the level of noise with the intensity of spiritual experience.

Prayers with visual aids or music

Prayer can be stimulated by visual aids or music and other audible sensations. Slides and photographs, or even sections from a newspaper can often provide a helpful starting-point. Listening to a song or even meditating on a few words may set off a whole chain of prayer.

Prayers with subjects suggested

In a group, sharing a topic or several topics can help to generate a sense of unity and freedom. Individuals can be asked to pray aloud for each topic on behalf of the whole group, or the topics themselves can be used to steer the spontaneous prayers of group members.

Prayers accompanied by actions

Kneeling or closing the eyes are actually 'action prayers', as are standing, walking, raising our arms... A whole range of actions can be used. Body language is a powerful way of praying for some people and, combined with music, it can lead to 'dancing prayers'. Something, it seems, is being accomplished through the physical action – another example of the physical having a spiritual dimension. The prophets, for example, did many weird and wonderful things at God's direction, accomplishing much through their physical obedience (see Ezek 4:1–5).

'Prayer walking' is another form of action praying, which involves individuals walking around a neighbourhood (with their eyes open!) and praying for perceived needs – for the homes, the shops, the schools, the community centres and the factories. Often God brings up issues as we walk.

Free-flowing prayers

In this form of group prayer, there are no 'Amens' at the end of individual prayers. Rather, one prayer flows into another. As one person finishes, another is prompted by God's Spirit to pick up on a theme from the previous prayer. It is as though we are going on a God-directed journey – travelling down the road, turning right, then left, stopping at traffic lights, going round a roundabout, and so on. Those who find it hard to speak their prayers won't need to worry if they dry up; they know that some-one else will take over. It can build a wonderful sense of togetherness in the group and be a time of special aware-ness of God.

Affirming prayers

This is almost the opposite to the latter. People are encouraged to think of another way of saying 'Amen' – for example, 'I agree', 'That's right' or 'I'm for that, too'. These phrases are written up and placed around the room. Then when someone prays, all affirm the prayer (assuming they agree!) by using one or more of the phrases – normally at the end of each prayer, but it can be encouraging if the comments are quietly spoken as the prayer is being given.

Simultaneous prayer

Here everyone is encouraged to pray or to express their praise to God, simultaneously! At first this sounded very strange to me, almost as though we were being rude to God – like children all trying to claim the teacher's atten-tion. But I soon realised that this was the wrong model. A more appropriate one would be that of a telephone exchange, where hundreds of messages can be handled at once. This style of praying can generate a wonderful sense of togetherness. Often it seems God will build faith and earnestness. People will be mutually sustained to pray over a longer period. For some, praying like this is like experiencing the exhilaration of the waves of the sea flow-ing over you. However, others may simply be bewildered.

Strategies to help us pray for all God's people

Prayer pairs

A prayer pair is two people committing themselves to pray regularly for someone holding a leadership position in their church. They do this with the leader's full approval and co-operation. Their aim is to pray consistently and sensitively over a considerable period of time.

To obtain the necessary information, the pair should contact the leader each week and ask for his or her prayer needs. Over the months the pair build a relationship with the leader, offering support and encouragement. Confidentiality is an absolute necessity. Sometimes it will be appropriate to feed back insight and inspiration to the leader, but never judgmentally and always in a way and at a time that is helpful to the leader.

Ideally, the pair should pray for the leader at least daily on their own and meet weekly as a pair. This time together is a good opportunity to seek for insight and for inspiration from the Holy Spirit. It cannot be overemphasised that the pair must function in a way that suits the leader and not vice versa. The purpose is to support the leader and to provide a service, not to add yet another task to the leader's list. So the pair must be prepared to be the ones to make all the arrangements and to pray without being thanked.

In setting up 'prayer pairs' in a church, there are many advantages in having someone co-ordinate the ministry. The co-ordinator's role involves working out with the leadership team of the church which leaders they wish to include in the scheme, and to sort out who would be appropriate to pray for whom. He or she will also need to sustain and coach the pairs. It is helpful if they meet each individual monthly, and if the pairs and perhaps some leaders meet every four months or so. This is a good opportunity to share any difficulties or joys, to swap ideas for helping the process to work, to give teaching on prayer or to recommend books that may help.

The co-ordinator is best placed to be the ears and voice for reconciliation. He or she must also be prepared, graciously and tactfully, to dissolve a pair or replace someone in it if their presence is proving to be unhelpful. Not surprisingly, it is vital that co-ordinators have their own pair praying for them.

Praying for people or groups in your church

Here is a sample of the many ways we can extend the circle of our prayers outward by building on relationships within our fellowship.

Make a list of the people you have prayed for recently. Some you will know personally; some you will like and feel close to; some will matter to you a lot; some will be important to the life of your church; some will have real needs for which you will feel compassion. There will also be those you find difficult to get on with! With all these groups, there is a link or bond between them and you. This will be a powerful motive for you to pray for them. Indeed, where there is a relationship (even a negative one), there is also a sense of responsibility which can be worked out, in part, through praying.

This list could form the basis for you to take the next step outwards – praying for your church. Perhaps you could start with task groups like the music group or finance team. Are there any groups that go unnoticed and unprayed for? Try to think of ways to encourage interest in them in the church and to obtain information on what they would like you to pray for. You could do this by putting up a collage of photos of the people involved with a diagram illustrating what they do; or write a short article with some prayer points for the church magazine. Or you could interview the group during a service, asking them for their prayer requests. People could be prayed for there and then, maybe with others laying hands on them as they pray. Over time, different groups or people in the church could be prayed for by the whole church. By establishing these relationships, there is the potential for networks of prayer to emerge. Home groups could be recruited to pray regularly, or individuals could pray at the end of a service.

Special occasions present further opportunities for

prayer. Try to think of creative and appropriate ways to share in special moments – birthdays, exams, illness, unemployment, promotion – and to initiate relationships that sustain prayer. Remember; quality of relationship rather than quantity is far more effective in stimulating prayer.

Perhaps for a month, or a week each month for a year, people could spend five minutes in a service with someone they don't usually pray for, and pray for him or her throughout the next week. Another idea is to organise a 'prayer carousel'. This works by dividing the church into groups of twelve. Person A contacts person B and shares her prayer needs. Person B prays for person A, but also tells person C what his needs are. This goes on round the group until the last person tells A what her needs are and person A prays for her. So each person prays for one person and is prayed for by one person. This can be done face to face, through notes or on the phone. Alternatively, a couple might be asked to adopt a group, and the group encouraged to meet with them regularly to share their joys and problems. This works well for people who are not so active physically, but certainly shouldn't be restricted to them.

But 'all God's people' is much bigger than the local church. Here are three ways to step out even further, using the same principles.

'All God's people' in our neighbourhood

If you discover other Christians living in the neighbourhood, you might want to consider getting to know them better. Then as relationships develop, you could support each other in prayer and share concerns for your locality. Why not arrange a coffee evening or hire a room at a local pub, and invite them along?

'All' our neighbourhood churches

Many of us find it hard work going to united services or even to other people's churches. Nevertheless, in doing so we will learn more about each others preferences and needs, and learn to thank God for each others strengths. Some churches find that adopting a personal approach is more effective in encouraging prayer. These may include running joint house groups or sharing in mission together, or exchanging ministers (or choirs or musicians).

'All' our network of churches

Another route to broaden our remit to pray for 'all God's people' leads us to our own network of churches. Whether yours is a 'New Church' or an Anglican Diocese, you can build on the link between you. Sometimes relationships between church networks seem remote and formal, but they can still be a great source of encouragement. You may like to consider joining up with another church for a year to pray for all the others in your denomination or grouping.

Into 'all' the world

Initially, it may seem daunting to realise that 'all God's people' does not stop with our county or country, but extends to the cosmos. But as we seek to broaden the scope of our praying, we can apply the principle we have already highlighted, of building on good quality relationships.

I have no doubt that God calls some people to a particular ministry of prayer for all the world. He seems to give these people special degrees of insight into the world's needs, and to establish a unique bond between them and the people or situation they are praying for. However, for those of us who are simply wanting to broaden our prayer life, here are some suggestions for a possible prayer strategy.

You could take part in a prayer strategy such as 'The hour that changed the world'. This can be supplemented by a country-by-country prayer guide, such as *Operation World*.[22] Simpler guides are also provided by many other mission organisations. However, accepting that relationships are the key to sustained prayer, perhaps using a world map would be a good starting-point – some maps even show the religious situations of major countries. Or use a map to plot times in different parts of the world – when people are waking up, working, eating, relaxing, playing and sleeping. Then thank God and pray for different people in different parts of the world, according to their activity at the time you are praying.

You could allocate a particular part of the world to various individuals or home groups to pray for. Later, they could share their insights and enthusiasm with the larger church from time to time, preferably on a planned basis. This could be at a 'missions evening' or as a regular spot within the main worship service. This will ensure that a comprehensive awareness of the world is maintained, fed by the insights and passion of those praying.

Another place to start would be to build on personal connections. It is amazing how many people have relatives in other countries or regularly make overseas visits for business or pleasure. There may well be someone in the church from another country. Why not 'adopt' such countries? Collect pictures, newspaper cuttings and/or samples of items they produce, and put them in a scrapbook. Are there any mission organisations working in that country? Can you establish a link with a church there? It can be a real boost for both churches when church members exchange visits.

Perhaps you know of someone working for a Christian organisation abroad, whom the church could 'adopt'. Write to him or her, send gifts for birthdays and share information, including service tapes. Then, when they come home, be ready to provide a 'spiritual home' for them.

There are other kinds of association worth exploring. Does your town or city have links with other countries, perhaps through the importing of raw materials as its manufacturing basis? What languages are taught in local schools? Many towns have 'twinning' arrangements with those on the continent. All such contacts can provide us with an ongoing focus for prayer. By praying for fellow Christians in these countries, we will be strengthening ties with them in a way pleasing to God.

Many of us have benefited from the ministry of people coming to the UK from abroad. American Evangelists like Billy Graham spring most readily to mind, but these days people from all over the world – Koreans, Latin Americans and Africans – are all working among us. On a 'March for Jesus' once, I walked alongside a person from New Zealand who was planting a church in Edinburgh, supported by people in Singapore! Globalisation is nothing new, however! If you are Anglican, perhaps the 'saint' after which your church is named hails from another country. Why not use that to stimulate your praying?

Prayer can be linked specifically to peoples' needs. It is here that a Bible, a map and a daily newspaper become our allies. We are called to pray with a Bible in one hand, a newspaper in the other, with one eye on the map and the other on Jesus. Perhaps a group of you could monitor a situation in a country and pray for organisations like the Red Cross or the United Nations, and for any Christians involved either as victims or as aid-workers. You could also establish a group of people to pray for needs that are not the media's 'flavour of the month'. The group could prod the church to pray for issues no longer in the headlines, and provide relevant information and insight.

To think about

1. If you are alone, ask yourself whether you find any of the suggestions in this chapter strange, difficult or even objectionable. If so, are you the kind of person who likes to break through barriers? Talk to friends from other Christian traditions and get them to take you along to experience them. Don't give up after one attempt! Talk through your response and compare it with those of your friends. It took my wife a year or two to enjoy Chinese food!

2. If you are in a group, read this chapter through and discuss the issues it raises. Talk about those aspects of praying that you find helpful and those you find hard. How can you help one another become more effective in 'praying always with all kinds of prayer'?

Endnotes

1. For those wishing to carry out more rigorous biblical study on the passages, the following books may be helpful: John R W Stott, *The Message of Ephesians*, The Bible Speaks Today, IVP, 1979; C Leslie Mitton, *Ephesians*, New Century Bible, Oliphants, 1976; J H Houlden, *Paul's Letters From Prison*, The Pelican New Testament Commentaries, Pelican, 1970; J Armitage Robinson, *St Paul's Epistle to the Ephesians*, Macmillan, 1903.

2. Warren Wiersbe, *Be Rich*, Wheaton, 1984, p26.

3. Prayer triplets are a method of praying in threes for friends to come to faith. They were initiated by Brian Mills for Mission England. See Brian Mills, *Three Times Three Equals Twelve*, Kingsway, 1986.

Prayer Partners are an essential element in the effective strategy of Evangelism Explosion. They involve people meeting to pray for someone involved in Christian ministry. For details about Prayer Partners and Evangelism Explosion, write to 228 Shirley Road, Southampton, SO1 3HR.

4. See Donald English (ed), *Ten Praying Churches*, Marc, 1989, pp43–46.

5. Paul Wallis, *Rough Ways in Prayer*, SPCK, 1991, p21.

6. Dick Eastman, *Love on its Knees*, Marshall Pickering, 1990, pp15–17.

7. For the argument that prayer in the Spirit has nothing to do with speaking in tongues, see J MacArthur, *The Believer's Armor*, Chicago, 1986.

8. Jamie Buckingham, *Risky Living*, Eastbourne, 1978, pp26,56–57.

9. Helen Roseveare, *Living Faith*, London, 1988, pp153–154. See also D Eastman, *Beyond Imagination*, Chosen Books, 1997, which has several illustrations of God's protection. A colleague in the USA tells how they were protected from a violent mob in India by an unusually well-dressed man who suddenly appeared and then disappeared. This person seemed to have angelic authority over the mob.

10. 'The Greek word for family (*patria*) is derived directly from the word for Father (*pater*) and ideally an English translation should indicate this close connexion' (Mitton, *Ephesians*, p132).

11. Roy McCloughry, *Men and Masculinity*, Hodder and Stoughton, 1992, p197.

12. Support for this comes from an unexpected source. Although Virginia Ironside considers herself a liberal agnostic, she recognises that the key value of prayer is to 'trust some other entity ... with one's problems'. She continues, 'being on one's knees is rather like being a cat rolling over on its back. It's a trusting kind of position, and the position itself may engender trust' ('Should I say a little prayer?', *The Independent* Review, p8).

13. Graham Kendrick, *Worship*, Kingsway; 1984, pp11–12.

14. Stott, *Ephesians*, p135.

15. 'If Christ dwells in the heart, it means that he controls that which directs the whole course of a man's life' (Mitton, *Ephesians*, p132).

'The Spirit comes to us not before but after we have accepted Christ and he comes as a Personal Companion to sustain us in our Christian Journey. When our minds suddenly seize upon spiritual truth and our hearts respond to a vision of God, and our lips utter prayers of breathless beauty, and our hands perform tasks of sublime service because we feel impelled by a power greater than ourselves – that is the Spirit of God at work in our lives. We do not have the historic Jesus but we do have someone to take his place' (Leonard Griffiths, *The Eternal Legacy*, Hodder and Stoughton, 1963, p101). Griffiths goes on to explain how the Spirit acts as teacher, authority, and helper – the very things Jesus was in peoples' homes.

16. 'The three hours of prayer in particular were so universally observed among the Jews of Jesus' time that we are justified in including them in the comment "as his custom was" ' (J Jeremias, *The Prayers of Jesus*, SCM, 1967, p73).

17. See D Brindley, *Stepping Aside*, Bible Society, 1993, for helpful suggestions.

18. For more detailed guidance, see G Kendrick and J Houghton, *Prayer Walking*, Kingsway, 1990.

19. J H Jowett, *The Silver Lining*, London, 1907 p183.

20. J R Larcombe, *Unexpected Healing*, Seven Oaks, 1991; *Beyond Healing*, Hodder, 1994.

21. A W Tozer, *Whatever Happened to Worship?*, Kingsway, 1985, p40.

22. Eastman, *The Hour that Changed the World*, Baker Book House Ltd, 1978; *Love on its Knees*, New Jersey, 1989.

Patrick Johnstone, *Operation World*, STL (which is regularly updated and available electronically). For access to missions, write to Global Connections, 186 Kennington Park Road, London SE11 4BT, informing them of your special concerns.